Simply Worship

MAUREEN LANG

KINGSWAY PUBLICATIONS
EASTBOURNE

First published 1983

This revised edition 1992

British Library Cataloguing in Publication Data

Lang, Maureen M.
Simply worship.—2nd ed.
I. Title
264

ISBN 0-86065-927-5

ACKNOWLEDGEMENTS

I would like to express thanks to my pupils who have encouraged me with their commitment and enthusiasm.

Thank you also to the sisters of the Community of Resurrection, Grahamstown, who gave me a quiet space in which to write the final draft and who nurtured my body and spirit while I worked.

Thank you also to my friend Janet Gordon who typed the script.

The demonstration tape could not have been produced without the skills, enthusiasm, commitment and humour of Robbie Penrith, Rector of All Saints Church, Roger and Beryl Hewitt, music leaders at St Cuthbert's and Estelle Kennedy-Good, English teacher and friend.

Finally, a deep thank you to my Bishop, the Right Reverend Bruce R. Evans, under whose authority I work and who supports me constantly in prayer.

Printed in Great Britain for
KINGSWAY PUBLICATIONS LTD
1 St Anne's Road, Eastbourne, E Sussex BN21 3UN by
Stanley L. Hunt (Printers) Ltd, Rushden, Northants.
Typeset by Nuprint Ltd, Harpenden, Herts.

CONTENTS

Please note that this book should be used in conjunction with the cassette
Simply Worship.

INTRODUCTION

The aim of this book

1. To encourage, train and equip Christians to learn to play the guitar simply but skilfully.
2. To link all the teaching of technique and songs to biblical principles of worship.
3. To incorporate musical theory as it relates to the guitar.

Why another guitar tutor?

This guitar manual offers four distinctive features not found in other tutors:
1. A short Bible study at the beginning of each session that links with the songs to be taught.
2. How to play specific songs that have been especially anointed by the Holy Spirit in the renewal. An emphasis is given in later sessions to songs by Graham Kendrick.
3. An introduction to melody playing.
4. Simple explanations of guitar musical theory, eg how C7 is formed and how it differs in structure and use from CM7.

How to use this book

If you are an absolute beginner the first six sessions give a basic foundation. The average person takes twelve weeks to reach this level.

If you have previously worked through my earlier edition of *Simply Worship* or know the basics, the first six sessions will be a quick refresher course before you start in earnest at Session 7. You will find that the first six sessions have different songs and some revised teaching.

A week's study means giving at least half an hour every day to practise. Use the practice record chart at the end of Session 1 to help you establish a routine and habit.

The intermediate and advanced sections include some optional theory and songs for those of you with the full biblical ten talents. I make it clear when you can omit these sections without weakening the course.

The Bible study in Step 1 of each session is an integral part of the course.

How to use the tape

The demonstration cassette is an essential part of the course. Many skills are difficult to communicate only on paper. I suggest that you listen to only one step at a time and practise and play *after* me at each stage. It is difficult to play along with a tape as the relentless mechanical tempo will quickly frustrate you!

The cassette has been recorded to an accurate pitch, but if your cassette player is a little old the pitch of notes may sound slightly low. This in no way detracts from its use as a teaching aid but does make it difficult to play along with.

Choice of guitar

The first decision is whether to buy a classical or a steel-strung guitar (otherwise called a folk guitar). The *classical guitar* is slightly smaller and lighter, has nylon strings and is best played with the fingers, not a pick. The *steel-strung guitar* is bigger, heavier and therefore more powerful. (Steel-strung guitars are available with six strings or twelve strings. Twelve strings are louder but more difficult to tune and play and so are not recommended for learning on.) You should be guided in your decision by where you are going to use the guitar. The classical guitar is beautiful for playing in a small room or with a house group, whereas the steel-strung guitar is better suited to a large church or youth situation. Try both types in a shop and pray that God will guide you in this first choice.

Do not buy a second-hand guitar unless you know someone who can check that the guitar is not warped or cracked. A guitar is very easily damaged. Do go to a well-known music dealer who carries a good range of guitars and ask the advice of the salesman who buys for the shop.

Choice of strings

1. Buy the correct gauge strings for your guitar—light, medium or heavy. Medium will probably be the best, but ask the advice of the shop which sells you the guitar.
2. Quality is geared very much to price.
3. Replace strings at least once a year, and more often if you are playing daily. When the strings are wearing out they become difficult to tune, will look slightly rusty and will lose their sustaining power.

Choice of picks and plectrums

Picks and plectrums are very much a matter of individual 'feel'. A plectrum is a thin piece of plastic which is held between the thumb and index finger while a pick actually fits on to your thumb. A heavy (that is thick) plectrum or pick is suitable for playing with a strong rhythmic beat, whereas light (that is thin) ones give a sensitive sound for soft songs or gentle picking. I have a medium pick for general use, but keep one of each of the others for special songs. Store picks and plectrums in a small box or make a cloth bag to hang on the head of your guitar; they are worse than pins for disappearing!

Other accessories

1. *A guitar case or bag*—If your guitar does not have a case, buy one if you can afford it. Cases are expensive but give excellent protection against heat and bangs. Second best would be a weatherproof bag with protective lining, but be careful of scratching the guitar with the zip. If you cannot afford either of these at the beginning, keep the guitar in the cardboard box supplied by the shop because this was designed to fit it exactly.
2. *Tuning aids*—It is not easy to tune the guitar when you first begin. Follow the instructions on page 15 exactly and buy one of the following aids:
    Tuning fork, a solid metal bar which when struck against a hard surface (or your knee!) will give a clear ringing accurate note. Buy one which is tuned to the note E because this is the same sound as your highest sounding string.
    Pitch pipes are easier to tune to because you simply blow the note for each string. However, unless you buy a good set you will not get a perfect match of note and will need to adjust the tuning as described.
    Electronic tuners are becoming available in increasing numbers and at reasonable prices. They all have different types of meters or flashing

lights to show you whether your strings are sharp, flat or in tune. Be careful not to depend on one at the expense of training your ear to recognise when your guitar's in tune.

3. *A ring folder*—As a supplement to this book you will inevitably collect other copies of music and notes. Experience has shown that the only satisfactory way to keep them without having a pile of wind-blown sheets all over the room is to put them in alphabetical order in a ring folder, preferably pasted on card so that they stand up on a music stand. Make sure that the folder will open flat. Be careful about copyright. Contact Christian Copyright Licensing, PO Box 1339, Eastbourne, East Sussex BN21 4YF for full regulations.

4. *A capo*—Later in this course you will need a capo. Capos fit on to the fretboard of your guitar, raising the pitch of the open strings. This means that you can use the basic chord shapes you learn here to play in more difficult keys.

5. *Guitar polish and oil*—I mention this because people are often tempted to use ordinary furniture polish on their guitars. If you do polish your guitar, use *only* the special cleaning materials a good music shop will stock. Always apply the polish with a soft cloth in the direction of the wood grain. For most of the time just keep the guitar clear of finger-marks by wiping it over with a slightly damp cloth.

SESSION 1

Commitment

Step 1: Bible study

Don't be tempted to skip this vital step! First of all pick up your Bible, even though you are burning to pick up your guitar.

Read: Romans 12:1, 6.

Question 1: What are you to offer first to God?

Answer: . . . .

Make this a prayer of commitment now, and don't forget to offer your hands.

We shall be studying a great deal about worship as we go through this course, but keep this following fact as a foundation principle:

GOD WANTS YOU FIRST ⟶ *totally loving Him*
⟶ *totally committed to Him*

Question 2: From verse 6, what are we to do with our gift?

Answer: . . . .

Believe that God has given you the gift of music and the gift of a guitar. Determine to *use* them for others. We are in His royal service.

Step 2: How to hold the guitar (when sitting)

Look carefully at the diagram and note:

(a) How the person is sitting—on the front of a chair without arm rests.
(b) How the guitar is kept vertical—not leaning back against the body.
(c) How the left hand thumb is *not* sticking out hooked over the neck—the thumb must be flat against the centre of the back of the neck.
(d) How the right hand plays over the sound hole.
(e) How the guitar is supported on the thigh and balanced by the right arm just below the elbow.

Step 3: Names of the open strings and tuning

Right from the start, resolve to learn the absolute basics of music that apply to the guitar. Diagrams help but your mind is part of that body you have just offered to the Lord.

The names of the six strings are given in the diagram below with a light-hearted rhyme to help you remember them. The 'E' or elephant string is the thick string nearest to you as you hold the guitar correctly and look down. It sounds lowest in pitch and in a packet of guitar strings is no. 6.

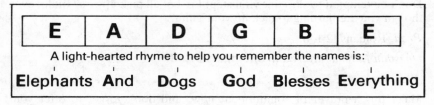

| E | A | D | G | B | E |

A light-hearted rhyme to help you remember the names is:

Elephants And Dogs God Blesses Everything

Play these six strings one at a time as described and demonstrated on the tape. If you have not been able to tune your guitar with one of the tuning aids described on page 7 you can tune it to a keyboard following the diagrams below. Otherwise, tune to the sound of my guitar as I play the open strings on the tape.

(i)

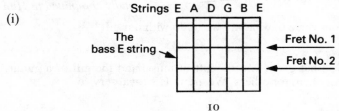

Strings E A D G B E

The bass E string

Fret No. 1

Fret No. 2

The following diagram shows how the open strings of the guitar are written in musical notation and where you can find the notes on a piano:

(ii)

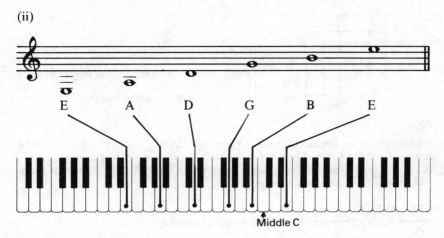

Step 4: Your first tune

The reason for learning a tune before you start to learn chords and songs is that it will help you to learn the names of the six strings in relation to music and sound.

1. Look at the notes in the 'clock' tune below and say their letter names out loud. Check with diagram (ii) above if you have forgotten their names.

THE CLOCK

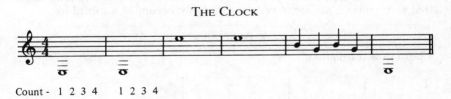

Count - 1 2 3 4   1 2 3 4

2. Listen to how the tune sounds on the tape, then imitate it. Be careful to count. The first four notes all last for four beats, but the black filled-in notes have one beat each. Imagine that as you play those black one-beat notes the clock is striking 4 o'clock.

Step 5: Your first chord of E major, first strum and song *Alleluia*

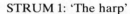
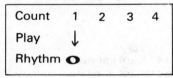

Place your left hand fingers where the dots are.

The index finger is numbered 1, the middle finger 2 and the ring finger 4.
□ = this indicates the string to be played first.

Strum 1: 'The harp'

Strumming is an important skill for the right hand. The aim is to make the strings vibrate evenly. Do not hit the strings but, rather like a harp player, draw out the beauty of the sound. You can strum with your thumb or use a pick if you have a steel-strung guitar.

STRUM 1: 'The harp'

Count	1	2	3	4
Play	↓			
Rhythm	○			

Abbreviations

↓ = a strong *down* stroke (towards the floor)
○ = count 4

Song Alleluia

This little worship song is very simple, but it is your first one so do not think it childish. The tune is the well-known traditional folk song *Frère Jacques*. Sing it with the tape before you play because this will help you to remember that your guitar is adding to your worship, not becoming a substitute.

ALLELUIA

Chord of E throughout

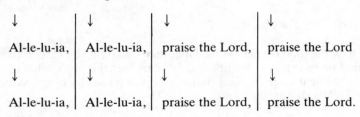

↓	↓	↓	↓
Al-le-lu-ia,	Al-le-lu-ia,	praise the Lord,	praise the Lord

↓	↓	↓	↓
Al-le-lu-ia,	Al-le-lu-ia,	praise the Lord,	praise the Lord.

How to play

1. Put the E major chord down with your left hand.
2. Strum down, using Strum 1, whenever you see the symbol ↓ .
3. Practise until you are perfect.

Step 6: The chord of A major and pick/strum style

This second chord of A major is one of the easiest ones to play.

Warning: the X over the bass E string means do *not* play this string. The reason is that you want the first sound of the chord to be note A—the name of the chord.

Strum 2: 'Pick/Strum'

This is a very useful strum for giving a strong steady beat. To play it you simply pluck or pick a bass string on beat 1 and strum down on beat 2. The secret of good playing is to pluck the correct bass string. You will probably realise this yourself, but make sure that when you are playing the E major chord you pluck the bass E string, and when you are playing the A major chord you pluck the bass A string. Do you see why I encouraged you to know the names of the strings?

The diagram illustrates how the strum is written. Listen to the tape for the sound.

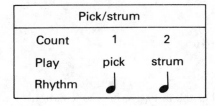

Pick/strum		
Count	1	2
Play	pick	strum
Rhythm	♩	♩

Now try this style to accompany the song *Alleluia*. Listen first to the tape.

Step 7: Practice record

This first session is certainly quite long, but now we reach the last step, number 7 the number of perfection. All your initial enthusiasm and interest will soon disappear unless you establish a good discipline of practice. Record your practice times on the following chart for a week and this will help you to fill in the questions below the chart.

PRACTICE RECORD

DAY	example	1	2	3	4	5	6	7
TIMES	7 – 7.30 a.m. 8 – 8.15 p.m.							
TOTAL	45 mins							

Questions

1. What is going to be my best time of day to practise?

....

2. How long can I really set aside?

....

SESSION 2

Reconciliation and Worship

Step 1: Bible study

Read: 2 Corinthians 5:17–21.

Question 1: Who takes the initiative in reconciliation?

Answer: ....

Question 2: Who did God choose and send to be His agent of reconciliation?

Answer: ....

Question 3: What great responsibility and privilege has He now given to us?

Answer: ....

Using your guitar in worship gives you a powerful tool to be an ambassador for Christ.

Warning: Read Matthew 5:23–24. Relationships quickly go wrong in guitar and worship groups, so keep checking that you are obeying the command given in these verses if you are disagreeing with someone.

14

Step 2: Beginning to tune the guitar by yourself

You will already have realised that if you put a left hand finger on a string at one of the frets, you make a note. If you make the note on each string which is the same as the next open string you can get your guitar in tune. Listen to the tape looking at the diagram below as you do.

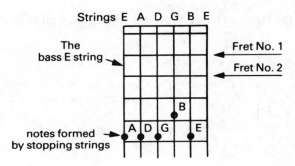

Step 3: Two new chords, B7 and E7

Later in the course you will learn how these 7th chords are formed, but music theory is best learned after you have experienced and *felt* it. For the moment listen carefully to the sound of these chords on the tape and how they are generally used.

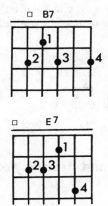

This is not an easy chord but one of the most important. When it comes in a song you will sense that it longs to move to E major so practise this change carefully and slowly all week. In fact many pupils take two weeks before they can change smoothly. The tape will help you.

Also note that you do not strike the bass E string.

Notice that this E7 chord is exactly like E major but the little finger is added to make the extra sound.

When you come to learn the song *He is Lord* in Step 5 you will need this chord to add emphasis and poignancy to the word 'dead'. Listen to how it sounds on the tape.

Step 4: Strum 3—introducing the 'up' stroke

1. This strum, which we will call Strum 3, uses an 'up' stroke which is abbreviated ↑.
2. This stroke is a light flick towards you (up) using a pick, or plectrum. If you are using your fingers you might like to try brushing up with the pad of your index finger or the back of the thumbnail.
3. Don't try to catch all the bass strings.
4. Listen to the tape and look at how this strum is written here:

Strum 3		
Count	1	2
Play	↓	↓ ↑
Rhythm	♩	♫

Notice that the 'up' stroke comes only at the end of beat 2.

Using Strum 3 with the song Alleluia

Put this new strum into use immediately by using it to accompany the *Alleluia* song from Session 1.

How to play

1. *Introduction:* Introductions are very important for establishing a strum and preparing the people you are leading. For this song, set the mood of joy by playing the strum strongly twice before you start to sing.
2. As you start to sing match your voice to the speed you have set with the guitar. I guarantee that everyone will join in with you even before you have reached the third word.

Chord E Strum

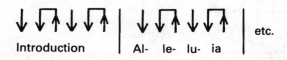

Introduction | Al- le- lu- ia | etc.

Step 5: Two worship songs *He is Lord* and *Peace is flowing like a river*

This week's two songs will help you to apply the new chords of B7 and E7 and give you more practice with Strum 3. Above all they will enable you to apply Step 1's Bible study on reconciliation.

He is Lord

The first three words of this song are one of the earliest creeds of the New Testament church, so again the beginning is important.

1. As an introduction play a single firm B7 chord.
2. Sing the first three words 'He is Lord' repeating the B7 chord only on the word 'Lord'. This will underline the strong credal statement.
3. Change to E major with your left hand so that as you reach the word 'Lord' at the end of line one you are ready to move into Strum 3.

Listen carefully to the tape to hear how the last two lines sound.

Intro:
↓   ↓   ↓ ↓↑ continue strum.
B7   B 7   E
He is Lord, He is Lord

                              E7   B7
He is risen from the dead and He is Lord.

              E   A
Every knee shall bow, every tongue confess

              E   B7 E-A-E
That Jesus Christ is Lord.

Author unknown
S.O.F. 36

I have taken care to teach you this song in detail because it is sung by Christians all over the world and you need to learn it even now from memory. This will mean that you can lead people into it at any time without relying on the music.

Peace is flowing like a river

        E
1. Peace is flowing like a river

B7   E
Flowing out through you and me,

E
Spreading out into the desert

B7   E
Setting all the captives free.

2. Love is flowing, etc.

3. Joy is flowing, etc.

Author unknown
S.O.F. 464

How to play

1. Practise the chord change E—B7 six times before you start every day this week. This change is the main difficulty in playing the song smoothly.
2. Use Strum 3.
3. As you reach verse 3 put more pressure into the strum and play right over the centre of the sound hole for maximum richness. You want to convey the sense of joy.

An original idea

Find another guitarist to play with and one of you play only the E major chord and the other only the B7. Not only will this remove the difficulty of changing chords but it will make you listen to each other carefully. As you share the playing and both singing, pray that the Lord will give His peace so that it can then flow from the pair of you to others.

SESSION 3

Joy and Skill

Step 1: Bible study

Read: Psalm 33:1–3.

Write down the three commands that are given in verse 3: . . . .

. . . .

. . . .

Some guitarists are very skilled, but they lack the joy of the Holy Spirit as they sing and play. Some guitarists are full of joy and enthusiasm, but their playing is so sloppy and insensitive it can actually detract from worship.

This week's work will enable you to develop skill and the songs will enable you to sing and play with joy.

But how do you play with skill?

We are not talking about learning 500 chords or acquiring great technique; we are talking about being a craftsman. This means knowing the Master Craftsman and playing every string and chord beautifully. Therefore:

1. Listen to yourself all the time.
2. Practise slowly.
3. Aim for beauty, clarity and control.

Give the Lord your best.

How do you sing and play joyfully?

Joy is a fruit of the Holy Spirit and can be there even when you are not happy. Spend some time praying for the Holy Spirit to live in you even more deeply.

Step 2: Joy and skill combined — song *This is the day*

You do not need to learn any new chords for this song. This means that you can consolidate the three chords of E, A and B7 and really be joyful.

THIS IS THE DAY

E
This is the day, | this is the day

    | B7 | E
That the | Lord has made, that the | Lord has made; |

E
We shall rejoice, | we shall rejoice

       | B7 | E
And be | glad in it, and be | glad in it. |

Use strum 3

↓ ↓↑↑

 A | E
This is the day that the | Lord has made,

 A   E
We shall rejoice and be glad in it.

  E | B7 | E
This is the day, | this is the day that the | Lord has | made. ‖

Les Garrett
Copyright © 1967, 1980
Scripture in Song/Thankyou Music
S.O.F. 130

Step 3: Strum 4, the simple 3-beat strum

This is a strum that will fit most songs with three beats in a bar. You will recognise such songs by looking at the *time signatures* in your music copies.

Right at the beginning there will be two numbers, the most common being $\frac{2}{4}$, $\frac{3}{4}$, $\frac{4}{4}$. The top figure tells you how many beats there are in a bar. We are looking at $\frac{3}{4}$ or triple time this week. All waltzes have $\frac{3}{4}$ time.

How to play

1. Count a steady three.
2. Move your right hand silently in the air as you listen to the strum on the tape.
3. Practise it yourself changing from E to B7 once you have got the feel. A good tip that works is to start changing the chord as you say 'and' after beat 3. Look below at the diagram and listen to the tape.

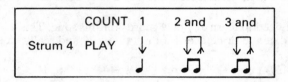

Step 4: Two songs using the 3-beat strum

THE LORD IS MY SHEPHERD

E   B7   E
The Lord is my Shepherd, I'll follow Him always.

               B7   E
He leads me by still waters, I'll follow Him always.

     B7   E
Always, always, I'll follow Him always.

     B7   E
Always, always, I'll follow Him always.

Author unknown

How to play

1. *Introduction.* Play twice through the 3-beat strum, starting to sing the first word of the song 'The' on the last ↓↑ stroke.

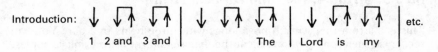

2. Which word always has the B7 chord to it?

Answer . . . .
This will mean you can quickly memorise the song.
3. Use this song with children but also with adults. It would be a perfect one for accompanying a Bible study on Psalm 23 or John 10.
4. Even though it is a gentle song, sing with the joy of commitment to Jesus Christ.

OPEN OUR EYES, LORD

   E   A   B^7 A-E
Open our eyes, Lord, we want to see Jesus

          A   B^7 E   E^7
To reach out and touch Him, and say that we love Him.

      A   B^7 E
Open our ears, Lord, and help us to listen.

      A   B^7 E
Open our eyes, Lord, we want to see Jesus.

Robert Cull
Copyright © 1976 Maranatha!
Music/Word Music (UK) a division
of Word (UK) Ltd,
9 Holdom Avenue, Bletchley,
Milton Keynes MK1 1QR, UK.
S.O.F. 275

How to play

1. Use this week's Strum 4.
2. Aim for a gentle but singing sound from your guitar.
3. Note that B7 always comes *after* you have sung 'Lord'.

Step 5: Test

You are now halfway through the beginner's section of the course. It is a good time to test yourself and consolidate before moving on. Any answers that you cannot easily find in the first three sessions will be given on the tape.

1. Write down the names of the six guitar strings

. . . .   (6 marks)

2. Which two chords do *not* use the bass E strings?

. . . . and . . . .   (2 marks)

3. Where do you play with your right hand to get the richest sound?

. . . . (2 marks)

4. Without picking up your guitar or looking back, name these four chords.
(4 marks)

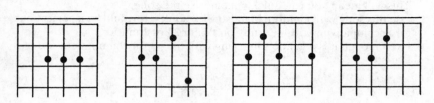

5. Complete the following quotations from memory:

(a) 'Play .... and shout for .... ' (Psalm 33). (2 marks)

(b) 'God was .... the world to himself in

.... He has committed to us the message of

.... ' (2 Corinthians 5:19). (2 marks)

(c) 'I urge you, brothers, in view of God's mercy, to offer your
.... as living sacrifices' (Romans 12:1). (2 marks)

My score....

If you have scored more than 15 move on. Well done! If you haven't, revise
these first three sessions.

Extra songs using the chords E, A and B7

HE'S GOT THE WHOLE WORLD

       E
He's got the whole world in His hands

       B7
He's got the whole wide world in His hands

       E
He's got the whole world in His hands

      A   B7 E
He's got the whole world in His hands.

2. He's got the wind and the rain in His hands, etc.

3. He's got you and me brother/sister in His hands, etc.

Author unknown

How to play

Choose yourself from Strums 1, 2 or 3.

LORD MAKE ME AN INSTRUMENT

```
        E       A   E                     A  E
Lord make me an instrument, an instrument of worship

        A   E       B7
I lift up my hands in Your Name.


Lord, make me an instrument, an instrument of worship

        E     B7    E
I lift up my hands in Your Name.
```

2. I'll sing You a love song, a love song of worship, etc.

3. Lord make us a symphony, a symphony of worship, etc.

Author unknown
S.O.F. 254

How to play

Only Strum 4 of the strums we've learned so far will fit this. Can you answer why?

SESSION 4

The Holy Spirit in Worship

Step 1: Bible study

The Holy Spirit is God the Father's special gift to us through Jesus, but a gift has to be received and used before it is effective. As we open our hearts daily to receive the Holy Spirit He will make the words of our songs, the melodies we sing and the guitar skills we use, alive, relevant and powerful.

23

Read: Ephesians 5:18–20 and then complete the following:

1. We are to be .... with the Spirit. This is a continuous infilling, freshly appropriated daily as we *wait* on God in prayer.

2. We are to sing and play first to .... and also to .... (see verse 19).

3. From verse 20 we can assume that many of our songs are to be songs of

....

Step 2: Minor chords, Em and Am

These are very easy!

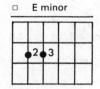

Step 3: Song *When the Spirit of the Lord*

This song uses your new minor chords, revises Strums 1 and 3, and relates beautifully to the Bible study.

WHEN THE SPIRIT OF THE LORD

Em   B⁷ Em
↓   ↓   ↓   ↓   ↓
1. When the Spirit of the Lord is within my heart

    B⁷   Em
I will sing as David sang. [*Twice, but keep Strum 3 going 2nd time*]

       Em
I will sing, I will sing,

    B⁷   Em
I will sing as David sang [*Twice*].

2. When the Spirit of the Lord is within my heart
I will clap as David clapped, etc.

3. When the Spirit of the Lord is within my heart
   I will dance as David danced, etc.

4. When the Spirit of the Lord is within my heart
   I will praise as David praised, etc.

Author unknown
S.O.F. 316

How to play

1. Introduction and first line use Strum 1 'The harp' as marked above.
2. Change to Strum 3↓ ↓↑ on the word 'sing' on line 2.
3. Allow the Holy Spirit to give your fingers, voice and heart the joy and freedom to sing for God.

Step 4: Chords D and A7

You have already learned the important chord of E and its related chords A and B7, and this group enables you to play many songs in the key of E. Now we turn to the chord and key of D which will equip you for another useful group of songs.

The chord of D looks easy but it only uses four strings, as shown below. The tape will illustrate how important it is to play only four from the beginning.

Step 5: Song *Father, we adore You*

Not only does this song use three of this week's new chords, it also reminds us of the Trinity: Father, Son and Holy Spirit.

FATHER, WE ADORE YOU

D   Em   A7   D
Father, we adore You.

D   Em   A7   D
Lay our lives before You,

D Em A7   D
How we love You.

2. Jesus, we adore You, etc.

3. Spirit, we adore You, etc.

Terrye Coelho
Copyright © 1972
Maranatha
Music/
Word Music
(UK)
S.O.F. 360

How to play

1. Use Strum 3.
2. Concentrate on playing the correct number of strings with the right hand, that is four for the chord of D, six for the chord of Em and five for A7.
3. Then aim for a gentle, smooth sound, always changing the chord as you strum 'up'. (You learned this in Session 3, Step 3.)

Step 6: Prayer song for the freedom of the Holy Spirit

SET MY SPIRIT FREE

A   D   A   D
Set my spirit free that I might worship Thee

E7   D   A
Set my spirit free that I might praise Thy Name

      D   A   D
Let all bondage go and let deliv'rance flow

E7   D-A
Set my spirit free to worship Thee.

Author unknown
S.O.F. 109

How to play

1. Use Strum 4.

SESSION 5

Persevering

Step 1: Bible study

This is the dangerous stage—the first flush of enthusiasm is over and the first difficulties are being met. It is usually easy when one is fresh and keen to begin any new task or skill. It is much more difficult to persevere when other demands on your time start to press in.

Read: 2 Corinthians 4:1.

Applying Paul's words for the moment to guitar playing, take a few minutes to dwell on this passage and these questions:

1. Who called you and gave you the desire to learn the guitar in the first place?

2. If you really believe this, what do you think is God's continuing role, especially when you do meet difficulties?

. . . .

3. What does Paul encourage *you* to do?

. . . .

Practical application

To persevere I suggest you do three things:

1. Keep looking at your goal; surely it is to be able to play the guitar with sufficient skill to enable you to worship the Lord yourself and to lead others.
2. Check your practice schedule and either adjust it or return to what you first decided was practical in terms of time of day and length.
3. Encourage and help one another within the class.

Step 2: The chord of G major (1st stage only)

You do need to persevere to learn the chord of G with the fingering I suggest. But if you learn it in two stages and really practise, this fingering will make more advanced playing easier. Most self-taught players adopt a variety of strange fingerings then later find it hard to make smooth changes to other chords.

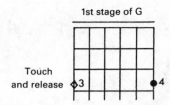

1st stage of G

Touch and release ◇3 ●4

Press the pad of your little finger (4) on to the string at fret 3.

(b) If you strum the top four strings of D, G, B and E you will have a chord of G major which is complete even if a little thin. Use it for quick changes or if you have very short fingers.

(c) But do try to work towards playing the full six-string version given in Step 5. As preparation, stretch your 3rd finger over and touch the bass E string also at fret 3. Release and touch this string several times as a practice.

(d) Then try the pick/strum style as on the tape.

Step 3: Picking style

Picking is an important skill for the right hand. To begin with each string is played separately, the thumb controlling one of the three bass strings, the index finger the G string, the middle finger the B string and the ring finger the high E string. Look at the diagram and notice how the thumb is kept in front of the fingers.

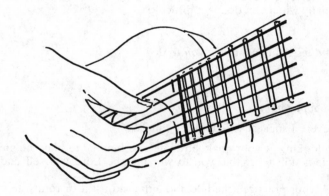

Now put down the chord of D with your left hand, rest the right hand thumb on the bass D string and pick each string in this order:

Thumb (T) on the D string

Index (i) on the G string

Middle (m) on the B string

Ring finger (R) on the high E

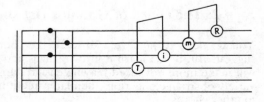

28

In future, the abbreviations for these fingers will be T,i,m,R.

Now listen to how I play with the thumb the bass string that matches the name of the chord. This is most important. The chords are D-Em-A7-D. If you can do that smoothly you will be able to move into playing last week's song *Father, we adore You*. Remember that it uses the same chord sequence. Listen to the tape.

Step 4: Song *When I feel the touch*

This lovely song is chosen because it enables you to use the picking style *and* the easy form of G major.

WHEN I FEEL THE TOUCH

   D   B7   Em   A
When I feel the touch of Your hand upon my life

        D   G   D A7 D
It causes me to sing a song that I love You, Lord.

         B7   Em   A
So from deep within my spirit singeth unto Thee

       D   G   D A7   D
You are my King, You are my God and I love You, Lord.

Keri Jones and David Matthew
Copyright © 1978 Springtide Music/
Word Music (UK).
S.O.F. 153

How to play

1. Use the picking style T,i,m,R. You will find that you can play it twice on every chord except for the changes A7—D on lines 2 and 4.
2. As you change the chords, concentrate on getting the left hand finger that touches the string nearest to you in position first. This is because you pick it first, of course. You do not need to wait until all the fingers are in place before the right hand starts.
3. Remember the Bible study. Since God *has* touched your life, He will enable you to persevere so that you *can* sing 'You are my King, You are my God....'

Step 5: The full chord of G major

Now try completing the chord of G by adding your 2nd finger at fret 2 on the A string. Persevere with this several times daily for at least a week. Only a few pupils fail to achieve this fingering and then it is usually because their fingers are very short. If you really cannot master this fingering try your 1st and 2nd fingers instead of your 2nd and 3rd.

Full chord of G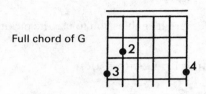

Step 6: Song *His Name is higher*

HIS NAME IS HIGHER

D   G   D
His Name is higher than any other

       A⁷   D
His Name is Jesus, His Name is Lord

      G   A⁷   D
His Name is Wonderful, His Name is Counsellor

      A⁷   D
His Name is Prince of Peace, the mighty God.

      G   D
His Name is higher than any other

      A⁷   D
His Name is Jesus, His Name is Lord.

Author unknown
S.O.F. 37

How to play

1. Use the pick/strum style for the first time of playing.
2. Change to Strum 3 ↓ ↗↑ for the second time.

SESSION 6

Completing the Beginner's Section

Step 1: Bible study

The main song this week is John Newton's *Amazing Grace*. Let us use it together with John 3:16 as a basis for our Bible study.

1. What one word did John Newton use to explain what had saved him?

2. John 3:16 is really an explanation of God's grace. If you complete the missing words you will be highlighting the meaning of God's grace which is really love in action.

   'For God so . . . . the world that he . . . . his one and only . . . .

   that whoever . . . . in him shall not . . . . but have

   . . . . ,

3. Beginning life as a fully committed Christian is rather like beginning guitar playing! One is enthusiastic at first and often the path is exciting. But difficulties and testing soon come.

   Question: What did Newton find in verse 3 helped in difficulties?

   . . . .

4. The final verse has much to do with worship, so read it carefully then answer:

   (a) The word 'I' which is used in verses 1–3 becomes . . . . . . in verse 4.

   This is because life and worship in God's kingdom is corporate.

   (b) What main activity does grace lead *us* to when we are in the kingdom?

   'To . . . . ' (last line)

   Once again, this is why you are learning to play the guitar.

Step 2: The last major basic chord, C major

Look at the diagram and note the points carefully

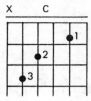

(a) Only five strings are played. Your 3rd finger on the A string makes the *note* C which is the base of the chord.

(b) Although you aim to put all three fingers down in this diagonal shape at the same time, think about the 3rd finger being placed first.

Changing from G to C

If you persevered in Session 5 with the fingering for G you will now start to reap the benefit. Change from G to C slowly and carefully and notice what little distance you have to move with the 2nd and 3rd fingers.

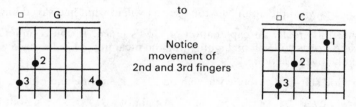

to

Notice movement of 2nd and 3rd fingers

Step 3: The chord of D7

This is easy to play and it is the 7th chord that 'longs' to move back to G. Notice that it has a triangular shape like D major but the point of the triangle is now away from you.

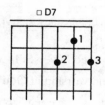

Step 4: Pivot fingers

Before we learn *Amazing Grace*, one more skill will now come easily to you. Change from the chord of G to Em, then from C to D7. Did you notice that each time *one* finger did not need to move at all? Do it again. These fingers which are common to two chords are called *pivot fingers* and it is important that you do use them as a pivot, not lifting them from the string at all. It enables you to move quickly and smoothly. Also notice that again it justifies having learned the recommended G major fingering! Are you convinced?

Step 5: Song *Amazing Grace*

AMAZING GRACE

```
     G                 C        G              Em         D-D7
1.  Amazing Grace! how sweet the sound that saved a wretch like me

     G                 C        G        Em        C  D7 G
    I once was lost, but now am found, was blind but now I see.
```

2. 'Twas grace that taught my heart to fear and grace my fears relieved.
   How precious did that grace appear, the hour I first believed.

3. Through many dangers, toils and snares I have already come,
   'Tis grace that brought me safe thus far, and grace will lead me home.

4. When we've been there ten thousand years, bright shining as the sun,
   We've no less days to sing God's praise, than when we've first begun.

John Newton (1725–1807)
Traditional

How to play

Use the 3-beat strum (Strum 4), keeping it smooth and regular.

Step 6: Picking style for $\frac{3}{4}$ time

This lovely flowing style has six sounds in three pairs of two. Look at the pattern below and listen to it on the tape.

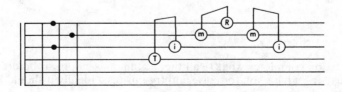

Step 7: Song *Preserve us, O Lord*

This beautiful prayer song could be used effectively at the end of a group meeting or in the evening.

PRESERVE US, O LORD

David McGregor Copyright © 1985 Thankyou Music,
PO Box 75, Eastbourne, E Sussex BN23 6NN, UK.

How to play

1. *Introduction:* one complete sequence of the picking style then enter with the beginning of the song on beat 3 of the 2nd bar as demonstrated on the tape.
2. Use the 3-beat picking style.

Test

This session completes what I call the beginner's section, so before you go any further I advise you to revise and try this test. Ideally it should be done with a teacher or fellow guitarist.

1. Name these chords *without* playing them:

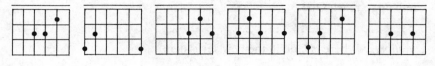

(6 marks)

2. Without looking at the above, play the chords in this order. Only give yourself two marks if you get every sound clear, one mark if you have remembered the shape and fingering.

   (i)   E   A   B7

   (ii) D   G   A7   D

   (iii) A   D   E7   A

   (iv) G   C   D7   G

   (v)   Em   Am   Em   (10 marks)

3. Write down the name of the chord which has only four strings
   . . . . (2 marks)

4. Choose two songs to learn and play from memory before you go on. (2 marks)

Score. . . .
Again, 15 is a good score.

SESSION 7

The King Is Coming

Step 1: Bible study

All the material in this session is based on three songs: *Tell me why do you weep?* by Graham Kendrick, *Open your eyes* by Carl Tuttle and *Lift up your heads* by S. L. Fry. Let us start then by lifting our eyes and catching again a vision of the new Jerusalem.

Read: Revelation 21:1–4.

Question 1: Write out a phrase that teaches us again that we *don't* have to climb up to reach God.

. . . .

Question 2: Where is God in the new Jerusalem?

Answer: . . . .

Now read aloud this verse from John 1: 'The Word became flesh and lived for a while among us. We have seen his glory' (verse 14).

Have you seen the glory of Jesus the King?

As you pick up your guitar and start to learn these songs, pray that you will see Jesus Christ in a new way—or perhaps even for the first time. He is a King worth serving.

Step 2: Chords D minor and B minor

1. ☐ indicates which string is to be plucked for the tonic or fundamental note of the song. Here it is the D string because the song is in D minor.
2. Look carefully at the fingering and number of strings to be played.
3. Remember that an x means you do not play that string.
4. Listen to each chord on the tape to train your ear to good sound.
5. Practise each one six times a day for a week. I guarantee you will then play them well!

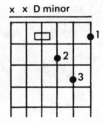

Bm: Your first bar chord

What are bar chords? Bar chords are the last major technical difficulty that your left hand has to master. The reason for them is that some chords need more stopped strings than you have available fingers, so the index finger has to press down more than one string at a time. But again, a determination and attention to detail enables most people to master them. Allow several weeks for real progress.

How to learn Bm

Work slowly, one stage at a time, looking at the diagrams and listening to the tape.

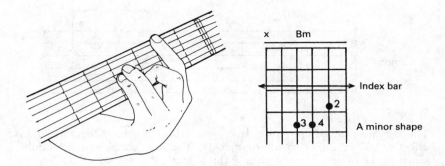

1. Place your 2nd, 3rd and 4th left hand fingers in the A minor shape at the 3rd and 4th frets (in other words, two frets higher up the fretboard than the A minor position).
2. Pluck these three strings slowly. You are actually making the three vital notes of the Bm chord. This shape and position is most important.
3. Lightly lay your index finger at fret 2—right up to the fret but not actually on it. You now have the correct hand position for the complete chord.
4. Try to get a clear sound from the notes under the barred index finger in this order:
   (a) The note under the A string. This note is B and the root of the chord.
   (b) The note under the high E string.
   Once you realise that you do not need to put pressure on all six strings with the index finger, the task is easier. Remember that the core of the sound still lies with the three fingers making the A minor shape.
5. Finally strum down the five strings, squeezing your left hand as you play them and then relaxing immediately. Count two beats then try again and do this several times. At first you may get little clear sound but gradually it will come.

Step 3: A new picking style, a new strum and song *Open your eyes*

It is now time to learn two new skills for the right hand. You will enjoy these after the hard work of bar chords.

New picking style

Instead of playing the fingers in the order T,i,m,R that you first learned, try this variation. You now play the ring finger second and it brings out the notes of the melody. Look at the diagram and listen to the tape.

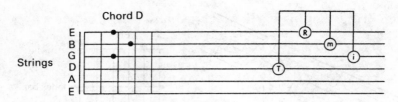

Chord D

Strings

E
B
G
D
A
E

Strum 5

This is a most important strum. It keeps a group of singers together and is effective played either slowly or quickly. The new element is the double *down* stroke of beat 3, so emphasise this slightly. Again look at the diagram and listen.

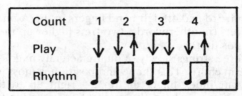

OPEN YOUR EYES

    D   A   G   A   D
Open your eyes, see the glory of the King.

    D   A   G-A   D
Lift up your voice and His praises sing.

G A   D G A^7 D
I love You, Lord, I will proclaim

G-A-Bm-G-Em A^7 D
'Alleluia', I bless Your Name.

Carl Tuttle
Copyright © 1985 Mercy Publishing/
Thankyou Music

How to play

1. The first time use the new picking style T, R, m, i.
2. Practise the change A to B minor separately and slowly every time you pick up your guitar this week.
3. Repeat the song, changing to Strum 5. It will give the impression of more people joining in with you in song.
4. Do not forget that this song, as with all of them, is chosen to relate to the Bible study.

Step 4: Developing earlier strums, and song *Tell me why*

People who teach themselves usually have a narrow range of strum patterns. The ones in this course are quite simple but they are effective for leading people in worship. The basic principle always is to use a strum that will best interpret the words.

Here are three developments of Strum 1, 'The harp', and the pick/strum style. They can all be used in the following song.

1. Elongate the single harp-like strum by playing diagonally across the strings from top left of the sound hole to the bottom right as you look down at the guitar. The symbol for this elongation is ↓ .

2. Use an alternating bass with the pick/strum style. Not many beginners manage to alternate bass notes but by now you should be able to do so. Very simply, the thumb or pick alternates between any two bass strings. The following are the best strings to use in these chords for this song.
   (a) For Am alternate on the bass A and D strings.
   (b) For Em alternate on the bass E and A strings.
   (c) For Dm alternate on the bass D and A strings.
   (d) For B7 alternate on the bass A and D strings.

3. Develop the pick/strum still further by doubling the rhythm of beat 2 like this:

TELL ME WHY

Am   Am
Tell me why do you weep? Tell me why do you mourn?

Am   E
Tell me why do you look so sad?

Am   Am
Tell me why don't you dance? Tell me why don't you sing?

Am   E
Tell me why don't you look to the sky?

39

Am E
1. Don't you know that your King is coming?

Am E
Don't you know that your King is nigh?

Am Dm
He is even at the gates of Jerusalem

B^7 E
He is coming on the morning sky.

2. Don't you know that the feast is ready;
Ready for the bride to come?
Brothers, keep your lamps a-burning.
The ending of the age is come.

3. Don't you know you are the Lord's invited?
Don't you know you are the chosen ones?
You in whom He has delighted
Shall rise with Jesus when He comes.

4. Come arise, my love, my fairest daughter.
The winter and the rain are gone:
The flowers of summer are appearing.
The time of singing songs has come.

Graham Kendrick

How to play

1. Use the elongated harp strum only on the chord name of the chorus.
2. On the last word of the chorus 'sky' change to the pick/strum style and accelerate.
3. As you reach the last word of the verse, again 'sky', double the 2nd beat of the pick/strum and return to the chorus.
4. For the purpose of this session's Bible study application, verse 1 and chorus repeated several times are excellent.

Step 5: Song *Lift up your heads*

This is easy to play so it means you can relax and enjoy worshipping the coming King after all the hard work of this session.

```
A        D    E      A
Lift up your heads to the coming King

              D         E    E⁷
Bow before Him and adore Him, sing—

A      D    E       A
To His majesty, let our praises be—

              D         E⁷   A
Pure and holy, giving glory to the King of kings.
```

Stephen L. Fry
Copyright © 1974 Birdwing Music/
Cherry Lane Music/Word Music UK.
S.O.F. 248

How to play

Use Strum 5.

SESSION 8

Training

Step 1: Bible study

Read: 1 Chronicles 25:1–8.

Question 1: How many musicians did King David set apart?

Answer: ....

Question 2: What two main qualities does verse 7 tell us they had?

Answer: ....

Question 3: Under whose supervision and authority were
(a) the basic musicians?

Answer: ....

(b) the three main leaders mentioned?

Answer: ....

41

Now think about your own training

1. In Session 5 you thought about your practice times. Training has to be daily, so think again how this discipline is going.
2. David's musicians trained and met together. Are you in a class or group where you can receive more training? If not, consider meeting with another guitar friend once a week for encouragement and help.
3. Look at the Contents pages for Session 8 onwards and ask yourself which areas listed there you really desire to improve. This will give you a goal and incentive. Write them down here:

. . . .

. . . .

. . . .

Prayer

'O Lord, enthuse me with Your Holy Spirit to develop and use the talent of music You have given me so that in the weeks ahead I will become a skilled, trained guitarist for use in Your service.'

Step 2: New picking style for right hand and song *I love You, Lord*

This style uses two strings together on the 2nd beat and is very attractive.

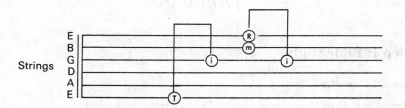

Listen to it demonstrated on the cassette and notice how even it must be, rather like a clock ticking.
Try it now to the song *I love you, Lord*.

I LOVE YOU, LORD

```
     G                     Am      G
I love You, Lord, and I lift my voice

      C  G  Am  G        D ── D7
To worship You, O my soul rejoice.
```

42

G Am G
Take joy my King in what You hear,

C G D D7 G
May it be a sweet, sweet sound in Your ear.

Laurie Klein Copyright © 1978, 1980 House of Mercy Music/Maranatha! Music/Word Music UK.

Step 3: New chords F# major bar chord, Em7 and alternative version of A7

F# major

The main thing to notice and learn is that it has the same shape as E major. As with Bm it is two frets higher so the index finger forms a bar at fret 2.

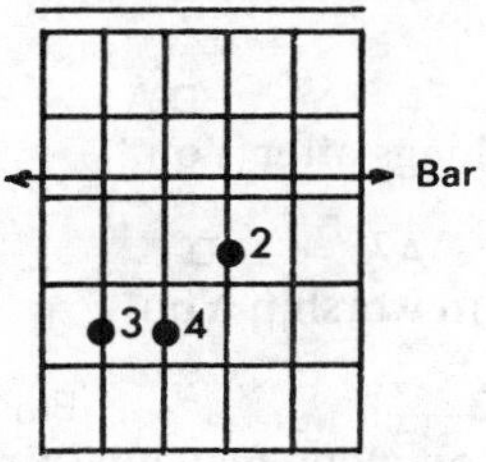

Remember to keep the balance of the hand over the 2nd, 3rd and 4th fingers that make the essence of the chord.

Em7

This week we are concentrating on training and skill so practise even this much easier chord carefully and start to understand what you are doing.

(a) First play the notes of the ordinary Em chord separately.
(b) Next add the little finger (4th) at fret 3 on the B string.

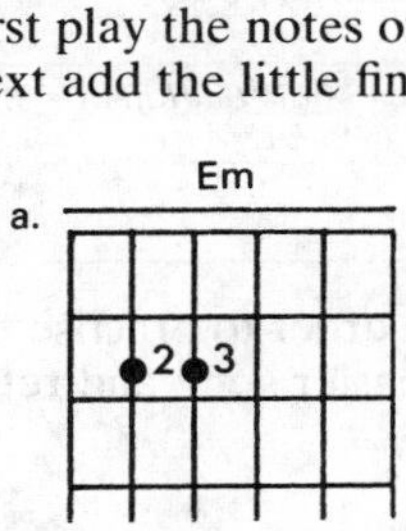

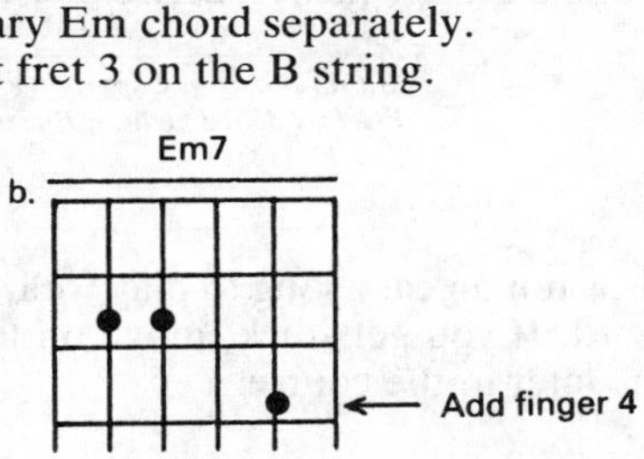

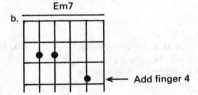

(c) Play the strings separately again and *listen* for that one altered sound on the B string. You are making the note D which is the 7th note from E. A fuller explanation of these dominant 7 chords is given as an optional extra in Step 5.

Note that many people play Em7 by leaving the bass D string open. This is not wrong and even useful at times, but on all 7th chords and other altered ones it sounds clearer to add the new note at a higher pitch.

A7 alternative version

All that happens here is that the 7th note of the scale of A, which is G, is played with the little finger at fret 3 on the high E string instead of using the open G string. Here are the two versions:

A7 with open G

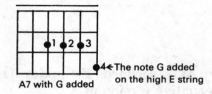

A7 with G added   The note G added on the high E string

Step 4: Song *As the deer*

AS THE DEER

D   A   Bm   G   Em^7 A^7 D-A
As the deer pants for the water so my soul longs after You.

D   A   Bm   G   Em^7 A^7 D
You alone are my heart's desire and I long to worship You.

Bm   G   D   G   Em   F#
You alone are my strength, my shield, to You alone may my spirit yield.

D   A   Bm   G   Em^7 A^7 D
You alone are my heart's desire and I long to worship You.

This is not an easy song to play well, but try it in order to practise the F# bar chord. If you get stuck, move on to the next easier song and return to this one later in the course.

How to play

1. Use Strum 3 ↓ ↓↑ until you are familiar with the chord changes.
2. Now try the picking style given in Step 2.
3. Another example of pivot fingers comes with the change of G to Em7. With all other chord changes improve your skill by going through the song with the left hand only (no voice or right hand), changing the shape *in the air* before you place it down on the strings. I tell children to think of their fingers as aeroplanes that change formation before landing. For

instance, when you change from D to A, go from a triangular shape to a straight line 'in the air'. Once you can do it slowly speed will be no problem.

4. If you are entrenched in the habit of putting down fingers separately, at least try to put the finger nearest you down first. If you think about it, this will be the sound you will need first when strumming down.

FATHER GOD I WONDER

   Em   D
Father God I wonder how I managed to exist without

     C   D   B^7
The knowledge of Your parenthood and Your loving care.

      Em   D^7
But now I am Your son, I am adopted in Your family

     C   D
And I can never be alone, 'cause Father God

     B^7
You're there beside me.

     Em   C   D   G
I will sing Your praises, I will sing Your praises,

Em   Am   D   B^7 Last chord Em
  I will sing Your praises for evermore [Repeat].

Ian Smale
Copyright © 1984 Glorie Music/Thankyou Music.

How to play

1. For the verse, use the new picking style given in Step 2.
2. For the refrain change to Strum 5 but now elongate the down stroke of the 2nd beat. It looks like this ↓↗↓ ↓↓ ↓↗. Listen to the tape for the sound.

Step 5: Explanation of dominant 7th chords (optional extra)

If you have no other musical knowledge you might find this step difficult, but it will add understanding to your guitar playing. Read slowly.

1. Dominant 7th chords are indicated by the figure 7 straight after the chord letter, eg A7.
2. The figure 7 is easy to explain. It simply means that you must add the 7th

45

note to the existing chord. The normal chord, as with all major chords, consists of the 1st, 3rd and 5th notes of the scale. The 7th note of A major scale, counting A as number 1, has the letter name G. Here is the musical alphabet in circular form to illustrate this.

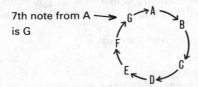

7th note from A →
is G

3. The difficulty comes with the word 'dominant'. In music this word refers to the 5th note or chord of a scale. A dominant 7th chord belongs therefore to the scale five notes *lower* and if you move anti-clockwise round the above diagram you will quickly discover that A7 belongs to the scale of D. This governs whether that 7th note of G has a sharp, flat or is ordinary. Since, in this case, the scale of D has a plain note G the dominant 7th chord. A7 also has just G, not G#. That is why you play A7 with an open G string.

Scale of D

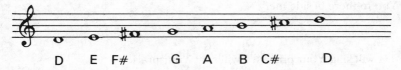

D   E   F#   G   A   B   C#   D

4. Underline the 1st, 3rd, 5th and 7th notes (remember D is number 1). You now have the names of the notes of A7. Write them here.

. . . .

Finally, look at them in a guitar diagram.

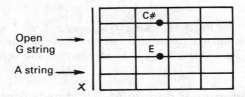

5. If you have survived and understood so far, try to work out the notes that will come in the dominant 7th chords of C, G and D because you meet these frequently. The answers are on the tape, but if you use the scale page in the Reference Section you should be able to discover them for yourself.

SESSION 9

Leading Worship

Step 1: Bible study

You may not be a regular worship leader, but there will certainly be occasions when, with your guitar, you will be called upon to lead a group. Let us see what 1 Chronicles 15:2,22,27 tells us about the musical leader who accompanied King David and the Levites as they brought the ark back to Jerusalem.

Question 1: Who was in charge of the singing?

Answer: ....

Question 2: Why was he given this responsibility?

Answer: ....

Question 3: What was he wearing?

Answer: ....

In Old Testament worship the wearing of linen signified the principle of dressing outwardly in a simple, pure material to cover the sinfulness of the person; it also showed his heart's desire to be pure and right before the Lord.

Application for us

1. In order to have Kenaniah's leadership qualification we also need to improve our skill in this session by learning some new strums and how to introduce and end songs.
2. Just as Kenaniah took care to dress in fine linen, we need to have the most important clothing talked of by Paul in Romans 13:14:

   'Clothe yourselves with ....'

   However, this spiritual application is no excuse for being careless about our physical clothing. It does not matter *what* you wear—clean jeans or a fresh dress—but your clothes are a non-verbal message to your group that you take coming into the presence of God seriously and desire an inner cleanliness of heart.

Extra study

If you would like to learn the interesting background as to why the Levites were in charge of temple worship, read what happened at the incident of the Golden Calf in Exodus 32:26,29, then Numbers 1:47–54.

Step 2: New strum for this session, the clock strum

I call this the clock strum because it gives a regular, steady accompaniment to songs with four beats in a bar.

While listening to it demonstrated on the cassette look at the diagrams below.

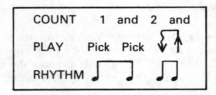

It has four separate sounds. The first two sounds are plucked on bass strings with the thumb or plectrum. The 3rd sound is the important one. It is a rippling *down*ward strum played diagonally across the strings.

The 4th sound is a lighter up-strum which needs only catch the treble strings.

Chord of C

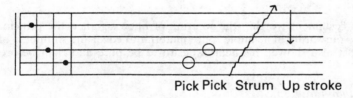

Pick Pick Strum Up stroke

Step 3: *Come into His Presence* using clock strum

1. I suggest different words from those printed in *Songs of Fellowship* for the first verse. For the purpose of leading people into worship sing 'Come into His presence singing Alleluia' then as verse 2 sing 'Praise the Lord together'.
2. You can play it with the chords given, ie D, G, A7. Later, when you have learned the chord of F you could play it in the key lower using C, F and G7. The former are easier to play, but if you are mastering the full bar chord of F this second group gives a stronger sound and is better pitched for a group.
3. Now listen to the song as Roger plays it on the cassette and try it for yourself.
4. Learn it from memory. It is a skill of leading to be able to look at the people you are leading and invite them with your eyes to come into His presence as you start to sing.

       D
1. Come in-to His presence singing

  G   D G   D A⁷   D

G   D G   D A^7 D
Al-le-lu-ia, Al-le-lu-ia, Al-le-lu-ia.

2. Praise the Lord together singing
Alleluia, Alleluia, Alleluia.

Author unknown

Step 4: Song, *Come bless the Lord*

I am using this song to illustrate introductions and endings and to use another development of the pick/strum style. This is a well-known song setting of Psalm 134 and is printed in *Songs of Fellowship*. For practice, play it in the key of E, ie using the chords in brackets without a capo. This will free you to concentrate on the right hand skill.

COME BLESS THE LORD

      F(E)   C7(B7)
Come bless the Lord all ye servants of the Lord

                             F(E)
Who stand by night in the house of the Lord.

        F7(E7)   Bb(A)
Lift up your hands in the holy place

        F(E)-C7(B7)   F(E)
Come bless the Lord, Come bless the Lord.

Author unknown

Strum

This variation of the basic pick/strum style simply extends it to cover four beats instead of two. Look, listen, try.

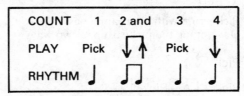

Introduction and ending

Both the way you play the guitar and the way you use your body will help to give a strong visual leadership, especially at the beginning and end of a song. You are wanting to attract people's attention to focus them on the words and then to invite them to worship. So...

1. Look up.
2. Invite them with your eyes and a smile to join you in worship (no need to speak).
3. Strike a firm single chord of E.
4. Sing the first three words unaccompanied then start the strum proper as you reach the word 'Lord'. I promise you they will join in!
5. As soon as people are with you, switch *your* mental and spiritual attention to the Lord. The best qualification for a worship leader is to be a worshipper.

It is also important to know when to end the song. Avoid always repeating a song the same number of times but be sensitive to the Spirit. When you do end, make it clear. Here is a suggestion for this song:
   Play the last bar plus one more beat as

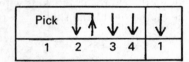

Make the final *down* stroke firm and definite, ie using three down strokes at the end. Be definite and know that the Lord is blessed.

Step 5: Consolidation of the course so far

It is fatal to rush ahead before each stage is consolidated, so take time now to look back over Sessions 7, 8 and 9 and check that you have learned all the strums, picking styles and chords that you did not know.

Checklist and test for yourself

1. *Chords:* Tick each one if you can play it clearly

   Dm   F#Major   A7
   Bm   Em7

2. *Strums:* (a) Pick/strum with alternating bass.
           (b) Developing the pick/strum in two ways:

           Pick ↓↑

           Pick ↓↑   Pick ↓

(c) Developing the basic ↓ ↓↑ strum to ↓↓↑↓↑↓↑ .

(d) Clock strum of pick pick ↓↑ .

3. *Picking style:* T, i, $\frac{R}{m}$, i.

4. *Songs from memory:*   Come into His presence
                          When I feel the touch
                          Come bless the Lord

5. Write out the musical alphabet ....

6. What does the '7' in the chord Em7 tell you?

7. Look up the answer Jesus gave to Pilate when asked the question: 'Are you a King then?' Jesus answered: '................................
....' (John 18:37).

8. Finally, enjoy worshipping the King with the lovely song *When the Spirit of the Lord is within my heart* in *Songs of Fellowship*. Play it spontaneously and only *afterwards* check how you played it. For instance...

(a) Were you using any of the new strums?
(b) Was your chord changing better than before you started this book?
(c) Did you develop the strum for the last two lines?
(d) Above all, did you believe what you were singing?

If you can answer 'yes' to most of the above, take it that you have passed the course so far.

Well done! Move to Session 10.

SESSION 10

Why Were We Created?

Step 1: Bible study

Read the familiar account of creation in Genesis 1:1–25. Use your visual imagination and write down four of the aspects that you love in God's created world:

1. ....   3. ....

2. ....   4. ....

By the end of the fifth day, verse 25, I feel that as God looked down at his new world his heart must still have been incomplete for there was nothing yet 'down there' like himself, no one to love him and tell him of their feelings of wonder and delight in his creation.

So, from verse 26, what was the decision of our trinitarian God?

'Let us make . . . . '

The story of the Fall follows on so quickly from the account of creation that it is easy to forget why we were created.

If you ask a group of people this question you will get many answers, all of them with some element of truth. In this brief study we will look at Scripture to discover from both Old and New Testaments what was God's main intention.

Read: Exodus 3:1–12.
Background: God is sending Moses to bring the Israelites out of Egypt. Besides being an historical event this is a prophetic picture of our salvation from the kingdom of darkness to the kingdom of light. But look especially at the purpose of their salvation. It was not simply to be free, happy, wealthy or useful, but to . . . . God (verse 12b). The 'you' in this sentence is plural; it does not just refer to Moses.

This purpose for God's people is also clearly underlined in Isaiah 43:21. The Lord says that the Israelite people he redeemed were formed for his sake 'that they may . . . . ',

We see the same reason given in the New Testament:

Read: 1 Peter 2:9.
You, the person reading this page, are part of the new Israel and you belong to God in his worldwide church 'that you may . . . .
. . . . ' (verse 9b).

The two main songs taught in this session are chosen because they underline this truth, but first let us see what lies ahead:

Sessions 10, 11 and 12 concentrate on an important group of new chords, another major strum style and the beginning of learning where individual notes are on the guitar.

In other words, I aim to teach you much more about the fretboard.

Don't be content just to follow diagrams. That is rather like a child colouring in by numbers, not very creative.

Even a simple understanding of how and why chords are formed will open up an exciting new world of sound to you.

Step 2: Chords Dsus4, D6 and D7sus4

What does Dsus4 mean?

Simply, the 4th note from D is added to the normal chord. That is the meaning of the 4. The word 'sus' is short for suspended and means that this extra 4th note is held usually for a short time before the normal basic chord is played again. So you will find that Dsus4 often leads back to D. (A book on musical theory will give you more information if you are interested.)

What is the 4th note from D?

Do you remember the musical alphabet? If not, look back to page 46 and counting 'D' as number 1 move to the 4th note.

At this stage you just need to check what kind of G this 4th note is. Is it ordinary G or G# or G♭? All the common scales are given at the back of this book in the Reference Section, but I have written out the first four notes of the scale of D here for you so that you can see what I am talking about.

D E F sharp G

Where is this note G on the guitar?

This is an important question and the first note that I am asking you to learn to read, both in music and on the guitar.

It is at the 3rd fret on the high E string.

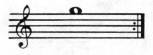

The note G in music

The note G on the guitar

Finally, what does the full chord of Dsus4 look like?

Look carefully at the diagram and you will see that it is formed by the normal D shape and the ◉ marks the position of the 4th note, G. I recommend you keeping the two fingers down on the E string because you then simply lift off the little finger to return to the basic chord. It also helps to fix in your mind how this chord is formed. I hope that you took time to understand that as well as learn the chord because it is fundamental to understanding all the other altered chords. I also hope that you agree it is easy to play!

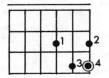

Note: Add the little finger without taking the 3rd finger off.

Song Make Way *using Dsus4*

This powerful and well-known song is often badly played by guitarists because they do not play the altered chords clearly. It is also important to play the following version of Am7 as drawn here.

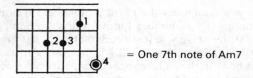

= One 7th note of Am7

Why *this* version? Because the 7th note of Am is also G, and this means that when changing to Dsus4, as you do no less than four times in the song, you can keep the same finger down.

Practise this progression now before you play it in the context of the song.

MAKE WAY

G   Am7   Dsus4   D
Make way, make way for Christ the King.

Graham Kendrick
Copyright © 1986 Thankyou Music

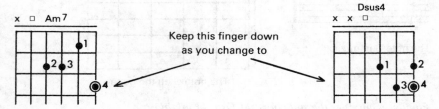

Keep this finger down
as you change to

The opening to the song is even more effective if you play the chord of G at the beginning with the fingering I gave you in Session 5 because you can then keep that little finger down for three chords in a row and the effect is smooth and clear.

The other chord you need for this song is D7sus4. The same reasoning applies. You put down the normal D7 chord and add the 4th note with the little finger. Yes, the 4th note is again G of course. So the chord looks like this:

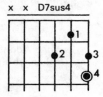

Now play the song, just strumming the chords and not singing, so that you can listen to your sound.

1. Use a bold uncluttered strum to start with: ↓ ↗↘ or ↓ ↘↗ .
2. Change to the common development of this for the chorus because it helps the echoes of 'Make way' to flow: ↓ ↗↘ ↘↗ ↗↘ .

Step 3: Chord D6 and song *How great Thou art*

The same principles apply, so you should be able to fill in your own answers quickly.

Question 1: What is the 6th note from D in the musical alphabet? . . . .

Question 2: Where is the note B on the guitar? Do I for instance have an open string called B? (If you do not know the names of your strings look at the first page of the Reference Section.)

Question 3: If I play the ordinary chord of D what do I need to do to make the open string B sound? (Answers are on the tape if you really are stuck!)

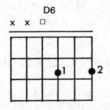

How to play the song How great Thou art

HOW GREAT THOU ART

```
     A                      D
O Lord my God when I in awesome wonder,

         A             E7       A
Consider all the works Thy hand hath made,

                      D
I see the stars, I hear the mighty thunder,

           A            E7        A
Thy power throughout the universe displayed.


         A7       A         D         A
Then sings my soul, my Saviour God to Thee,

           E7                     A
How great Thou art, how great Thou art,
```

A⁷　　　　D　　　　　A
Then sings my soul, my Saviour God to Thee,

D⁶　　　　　　A
How great Thou art, How great Thou art.

Stuart K. Hine
Copyright © 1953 Stuart K. Hine/
Thankyou Music.

The decision how to play this song needs to be partly governed by who is singing it. Here are some suggestions:

1. To accompany a *soloist* for verse 1 while people really meditate on creation is a good idea, especially if outdoors. In this case use the single harp-like strum ↓ changing to the picking style T, i, $\frac{R}{m}$, i on the word 'made'. Listen to the tape as I accompany Beryl.
2. If accompanying a *group* start with an uncluttered strum—either the basic ↓ ♫ strum or the clock strum.
3. In both cases change as you reach the last word of the verse, 'displayed'. Doing this really lifts the whole song into the response of joy...'Then sings my soul'.

Step 4: Relating the songs to the Bible study on creation

Instead of moving on to new work, the last part of this session is written to encourage you to look back at the Bible study. Can you see how the songs illustrate the teaching?

In *How great Thou art* the first two verses dwell on aspects of God the Creator (the stars, birds, mountains) and the worship response in the chorus is praise.

In *Make Way* full attention is focused on Jesus Christ and the tremendous transformation he brings to our lives. The worship response comes in verse 4—'We call you now to worship Him'.

Optional extra song for this week, Shine, Jesus, shine

The chord changes here are quick, but this well-known song of Graham Kendrick's combines praise, proclamation and prayer in a wonderful way.

SHINE, JESUS, SHINE

A　　　　　　D　　　　A　Bm　　　　　E
Shine, Je-sus, shine,—fill this land with the Father's glory

A　　　　　　D　　　　A　Bm　　　G-E
Blaze, Spi-rit, blaze,—set our hearts on fire.

56

SESSION 11

Christian Worship

Step 1: Bible study

Many books and definitions have been written in an attempt to answer the question: 'What is Christian worship?'—the question which men of all time seek to explain because it stirs their innermost being.

It stirs our innermost being because worship is what we were designed to do—and worship is what we *do* do—though too often the object of our worship is an idol of money, person, possessions or self. But worship still remains elusive if we try to define it because our minds are finite and God, the true object of our worship, is infinite. We cannot box God, we cannot reduce him or our response to him to a definition, and this is marvellous because if we could do this worship would lose its essential element of mystery.

But surely the Bible will define worship for us? The answer is 'no' in the sense that there is not a neat definition which starts 'Worship is...'. Yet in the Bible we do find stories of men worshipping God and pictures of the glory of the worship in heaven. From a study of all this we can attempt a definition. Let us take two examples:

Read: Isaiah 6:1–8 and Revelation 4:1–11.

Question 1: Tick the correct statement
(a) Isaiah and John worshipped God and he then appeared.
(b) God appeared and then Isaiah and John worshipped.
    Yes, God always takes the initiative by revealing himself, *then* man responds. The worship response can be singing, tears, dancing or thanksgiving.
    So consider this definition: *Worship is our response to some revelation of God.*

57

Question 2: Is this a sufficiently comprehensive definition for describing Christian worship?

Answer: . . . .

If you think deeply, Christian New Testament worship is different from Old Testament. The awe and majesty are still there, but there is a joy and depth not met in any other religion's worship of God because we know that in Jesus Christ we have the full revelation of God and his saving love for us. When Thomas saw the crucified, risen Christ he said: '. . . . .' (John 20:28).

So consider this full definition of Christian worship: *Christian worship is our response to the revelation of God's love in Jesus Christ.*

When you have time, read the book of Revelation, that book of the Bible which gathers the whole epic of God's salvation together and shows us the present and future glory of the Trinity perfectly revealed and restored.

Here we have incomparable pictures of worship. Soak yourself in the sounds, scents and images that John, with the limitation of language, uses to paint mankind and creation responding to God and the Lamb. Then you need no longer ponder the question: 'What then is worship?' You will have a heart and spirit understanding that will transcend words, but which will lead you to . . . simply worship.

Step 2: Major 7th chords

Have your pencil and guitar ready to work through this next learning unit and the tape recorder close at hand to listen to examples. Many guitarists still confuse a chord such as D7 with DM7. The capital 'M' in DM7 stands for the word 'major'. This chord can also be written as Dmaj7.

You have already learned that chords such as D7 are called dominant 7ths and come from the scale or key five notes lower.

These major 7th chords have a much simpler explanation. Just like D4 or D6 they are formed by adding the 7th note of the major scale to the existing chord.

Work through the following exercise. The scales of D and A major are written out to help you.

1. Dmaj7—formed from the scale of D major

D E F# G A B C# D

Learn where the 7th note is in music.

58

(a) What is the 7th note from D?

(b) After looking at the plan of the first three notes of the B string describe where this 7th note of C# is to be found.

Strings E A D G B E

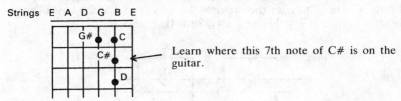

Learn where this 7th note of C# is on the guitar.

(c) Draw Dmaj7 on this empty plan.

1. First put in the dots for D major using a *pencil*.
2. Next put an ⦿ for the C# 7th note. This time you will have to rub out one of the D major chord notes so that the C# sounds clearly. But doing it this way will show you the construction of the new chord.

(d) Listen to it on the cassette and then play it for yourself. Remember that it will only use four strings since it belongs to the 'D' family. When practising it, as with *all* new chords, play it with separate sounds *slowly*, then strum it using the ↓ strum.

Step 3: *Jesus, Name above all names* using Dmaj7 and new picking style

This song is taken from *Songs of Fellowship*, but I have written it out below with different chords. They are very effective and use this new Dmaj7th. The accompaniment is lovely. There are *three* sounds to every beat. In music this is called a triplet. So the guitar needs to follow this rhythm.

How to play

1. Using the right hand in picking style listen and then try this to the chord of D

Strings

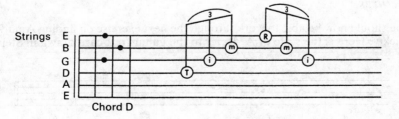

Chord D

59

2. Play this pattern twice for the 1st bar, then change to Dmaj7 and play it twice again for the 2nd bar. Carry on with Em7 for the 3rd bar.
3. When you come to the 4th bar which has the one word 'Lord' but four chords, you need to alter the order of the fingers so that the bass of each chord is sounded. Try this on each chord. It is easy!

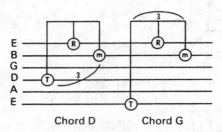

Chord D   Chord G

4. You should all manage this song easily, so commit it to memory and relate it to the Bible study. In other words, worship Jesus while you play and sing.

JESUS, NAME ABOVE ALL NAMES

D   Dmaj7
Jesus, name above all names,

          Em7   D-G-D-A
Beautiful Saviour, Glorious Lord;

          D   Dmaj7
Emmanuel, God is with us,

          Em7   D-G-D
Blessèd Redeemer, Living Word.

Naida Hearn Copyright © 1974, 1979
Scripture in Song/Thankyou Music

Step 4: Chords Amaj7, Esus4 and D/A and song *All heaven declares*

You should now be able to work through the next exercise on finding Amaj7 quickly. Here is the scale of A. Refer to the guitar fretboard drawn in Step 2.

1. What is the 7th note from A? ....
2. Describe where it is on the fretboard.

   It is at the .... fret on the .... string.

So it will look like this:

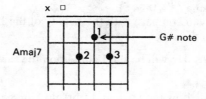

Amaj7 — G# note

Play it after listening to the cassette.

Chord Esus4

This will include the 4th note from E which in the musical alphabet is ....
Although you do have an A string, remember that it is better to *add* the 4th
note.

Refer to the fretboard diagram below and you will see that the note A is
on the .... string at the .... fret.

So this is a similar playing approach as to Dsus4. Put down the normal
chord of E and add your little finger to make the note A.

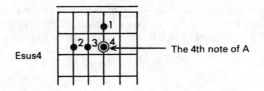

Esus4 — The 4th note of A

Chord D/A

This introduces another series of altered chords, in this case those with
altered bass notes.

First let me explain what the symbol D/A means. The first letter, D, tells
you that it is based on the chord of D. The 'A' after the slash means you
must include the bass note of A.

This chord is an easy example because you *do* have an open A string. So
when you see this instruction, you play five strings so as to catch the sound
of A. But be careful... you still do not catch the bass E string.

NB Some of these altered bass chords are not easy to play on the guitar.
For instance, E/G which comes in the next song, *All heaven declares*. In
these cases it is better to keep to the normal chord and the keyboard player
or bass guitarist will emphasise the altered bass note.

ALL HEAVEN DECLARES

A   Amaj⁷   D-E⁴   E   D/A A
All heav'n declares the glory of the risen Lord,

A   Amaj⁷ D-E4 E   D/A   A
Who can compare with the beauty of the Lord?

A   D-E   A —— E
Forever He will be the Lamb upon the throne.

F#m   D-E7   A-D/A-A
I gladly bow the knee and worship Him alone.

Noel and Tricia Richards
Copyright © 1987 Thankyou Music.

1. I suggest the strum ↓↓↑↓↓↓↑ to start with. After you have learned the syncopated strum in the next session you could use that.
2. For F# minor refer to Session 12.

Hint for leading worship

This week's songs concentrate on Jesus Christ. Have the Bible study on the definition of Christian worship firmly in your mind.

To convey this to the people you are leading be wary of giving them a 'lecture' in the middle of worship—keep that for a Bible study. But if you are actually responding to Jesus as you play, the Holy Spirit will communicate this to the people and they will also be drawn to him.

SESSION 12

Holy Ground

Step 1: Bible study

In house churches or small group meetings the place, perhaps a bare hall or television-dominated living room, sometimes makes it difficult for Christians to worship easily. Yet only one truth needs to be brought home to us. See if you can discover it for yourself in these three readings: Genesis 28:10–17 (especially verse 17); Exodus 3:1–5 (especially verse 5); Matthew 18:20.

Questions:

1. How do you think Jacob viewed the place where he had to sleep in Genesis 28:11? ....
....

2. How had his attitude changed when he woke up in verse 17? ....
....

3. What had made the difference? ....

4. In what kind of geographical place was Moses in Exodus 3?
....

5. How did God describe the same place in verse 5? ....
....

6. Why was it? ....

7. What is the tremendous truth for Christians in Matthew 18:20?
....

Respond now

Wherever you are reading this—even if it is in a shop, train or bedroom— stop reading, realise Christ is with you and worship him. When you have learned the song *Be still* in Step 5, come back to this study and sing it in the Lord's presence.

Step 2: Chords Asus4, Gsus4, F#m and C#m (easy version)

Asus4 and Gsus4 are the next two common suspended 4th chords to learn. The same principles apply as with D and Esus4ths. I hope you are getting excited about understanding *how* these chords are formed. Use the scales printed in the Reference Section for these exercises. They are written at the pitch that will give you the best 4th notes on the guitar.

Questions

1. What is the 4th note from A? ....

2. Where is this note on the fretboard?

    It is on the .... string at the .... fret.

63

3. Draw the normal chord of A major on the diagram and add with an ⊙ the position of this 4th note D (finger 4).

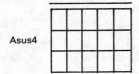

Asus4

Check with Summary of Chords, page 123.

Now do the same for Gsus4.

4. What is the 4th note from G? ....

5. Where is this note on the fretboard?

   It is on the .... string at the .... fret.

6. Draw the normal chord of G and add with an ⊙ the position of this note C on the B string. It is played with your index finger 1—another reason for having learned the G fingering I recommend in Session 5.

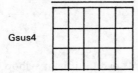

Gsus4

C#minor (easy or inverted version) and F#minor

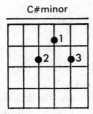

C#minor

Note the similarity to AM7 but in this case do not play the bass A string. Later we will learn the full bar version.

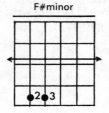

F#minor

You could play a half bar by omitting the 2nd finger and playing just four strings.

Step 3: Important new strum—the syncopated strum

Remember that one of the dangers any guitarist can fall into (and I do myself) is to play the same narrow range of strums for every song we sing. You DO need a few basic outlines, but on these you develop variations. My aim is to show you some of these variations and then encourage you to try your own. The Reference Section summarises the basic strums with their variations.

The syncopated strum is a very good one and I really recommend it. So take your time. Read the explanation carefully, listen to the examples on the tape and try each stage for yourself.

What does the word 'syncopated' mean in music?

It simply means that an expected sound is missed out. The missed sound is shown in music either by writing a *rest*, eg **ʹ** , indicating silence or by tying two notes together with a little line like this:

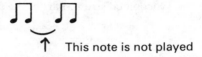

↑ This note is not played

What does it look like in guitar symbols?

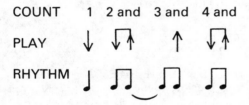

How do I play it?

Two preliminary exercises help many people:

1. Turn the tape on and listen to the strum. At the same time, hold your guitar and move your hand a little distance from the strings playing silently 'in the air' without making a sound. This allows you to get the feel of the strum as you 'play' with the tape.
2. Speak out loud what you are doing in terms of direction, slowing down the strum. Slowly say as you play: 'Down/down/up—Up/down/up.' Join with me on the tape.

You may on the other hand be one of those gifted people who can pick it up straight away just by listening.

Finally, what is the main use of this strum?

The accent which normally comes quite strongly on the 3rd beat is thrown on to a weaker note and so fast songs gain a drive and impulse forward, and slow songs somehow have a controlled, relaxed feeling. Listen as Roger and Robbie demonstrate the beginnings of the two songs *Our God reigns* for a fast example, and *Lord You are so precious to me* for a slow one.

NB: the song *Our God reigns* is taught fully in the next session.

Step 4: Song *Lord You are so precious to me*

How to play

1. First of all play it in the original key of A, ie with no capo. I always do with this song. Not only will it give you the satisfaction of using the new easy C#minor very effectively, but you will also get extra practice with Esus4 and an introduction to playing Asus4 which you worked out in Step 2.
2. Use the new syncopated strum. Part of the song is now demonstrated on the tape.

(Optional)

3. Try it again with the capo at fret 2. This means you can use the new Gsus4.

LORD YOU ARE SO PRECIOUS TO ME

A   C#m   D   Esus4-E
Lord, You are so precious to me,

A   C#m   D   Esus4-E
Lord, You are so precious to me

      D   E   A   F#m
And I love You, yes, I love You

   D   E   A-Asus4-A
Because You first loved me.

Graham Kendrick
Copyright © 1986 Thankyou Music

Step 5: Song *Be still*

How to play

This is a song which lends itself to several possibilities depending on the size of the group and your own 'feel'. So the following are only suggestions:

1. To accompany a soloist or small group, use finger picking style:
   T, i, $\frac{R}{m}$, i.
2. Also for a small group, and if you prefer a pick, use the clock strum.
3. For a bigger group, do not despise the steady basic ↓ ↓↑ strum.
4. Combine two strums by using the basic style in point 3, but syncopating the long notes, such as on the word 'here'.

In *all* cases try emphasising the whole purpose of the song (that is, to be still) by playing the first bar of the *last* line of each verse with two simple single but strong down strums. Listen to the tape.

BE STILL

 D   F#m   Bm Em⁷   A
 Be still, for the presence of the Lord, the Holy One is here.

 D   F#m Bm Em⁷   Asus4-A
 Come bow before Him now, with reverence and fear.

 G A D   G   A   D
 In Him no sin is found, we stand on holy ground.

 G A   F#m   Bm   Em7 Asus4-A D
 Be still, for the presence of the Lord, the Holy One is here.

Dale Evans
Copyright © 1986 Thankyou Music

Test on Sessions 10, 11 and 12

1. Name these notes on the fretboard:

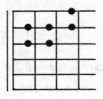

(6 marks)

2. Name these notes in music:

(4 marks)

3. Name these chord shapes (⊙ = an added note):

(4 marks)

4. Complete this definition of Christian worship: 'Christian worship is our

   . . . . . . to the revelation of God's . . . . in . . . .' (3 marks)

5. Biblically speaking a place is made holy by the presence of . . . .

   . . . . (2 marks)

I do not advise you to go further until you can get $\frac{15}{20}$ without looking up the answers or listening to them on the tape.

SESSION 13

How Many Talents Do You Have?

Step 1: Bible study

First of all, answer these questions. They will help you to refocus on why you are studying this book.

1. In the last month, has the guitar been mostly unopened in my case or

   taken out regularly for playing and practice? . . . .

2. If I have been playing, has it been

   (a) to practise? ☐

   (b) to play in ministry—either ministering to the Lord in my own worship, leading a group, or playing as part of a team? ☐

   (c) both for practice and ministry? ☐

3. How many talents do I honestly think I have been given for this instrument?

   one ☐   two ☐   five ☐   (often a Christian friend or teacher will give you a more honest assessment than you can)

Now read Matthew 25:14–30.

4. How many talents did the servant have who displeased the Lord? . . . . .

5. Why? . . . .

6. How did the two and five talent servants please Jesus? . . . .

Application—to encourage you now

In eleven years of teaching this instrument in group situations my experience has been:

1. Fewer than ten people have given up because they simply did not even have one talent. In other words, if you got as far as buying a guitar and a book the very desire was probably a sign that God has given some talent.
2. Lack of good progress is usually unrelated to the number of talents but more to
   (a) Laziness in daily practice (quite often the five-talent people).
   (b) Lack of commitment to the calling and gift.
   (c) A genuine over-commitment to many Christian activities and the need to reassess where God was wanting to use them at that time.
   (d) Age! Unfortunately, after the age of forty fingers do start to stiffen, but progress will just be slower.
3. Those who flourished in their playing, including some one-talent people, usually did so because they both practised and *used* their guitar in ministry. The ministry might only be at the level of playing to their children, but this is very valuable. In fact I can think of three pupils who definitely only had one talent, but who were on fire for the Lord and practised hard and who are now playing regularly in groups.

Prayer

'Lord, thank you for my . . . . . . talent(s) [fill in how many you discern you have]. Forgive me for neglecting it(them). Please let your Holy Spirit act upon my intention to practise regularly and continue with this course.'

Step 2: Using your talent(s)—two easy and well-known songs for extra practice with the syncopated strum

Song: Rejoice in the Lord always

The music for this can be found in *Songs of Fellowship*, but I have given it here with simple chords so that you can concentrate on the strum.

E   B^7 E
Rejoice in the Lord always and again I say rejoice (twice)

E   B^7 E
Rejoice, rejoice, and again I say rejoice (twice).

Evelyn Tarner
Copyright © 1967 Sacred Songs/Word Music (UK).

How to play

The syncopated strum with drive and joy.

Song: Our God reigns

Using capo at fret 1 as indicated.

How to play

1. The syncopated strum again.
2. Start with the refrain as on the cassette because it is straightforward in its use of the strum.
3. The verses present a possible problem which you will meet with in all more advanced strums. This comes when you have more than one chord in a bar. In this song where you have two chords at the end of a bar, eg D and A on the words 'brings good', play a single strong *down* strum on each like this: ↓ ↓

Where the two chords come on the 1st and 3rd beats, eg 'feet of Him', don't analyse how to fit the strum to the words. Just keep the right hand going with the strum, changing the chords on the right beat and allow the people to sing over you. It is then no problem!

OUR GOD REIGNS

A   D   E   D A
How lovely on the mountains are the feet of Him
  D   A Bm E   A
Who brings good news, good news,
       D   E   D A
Proclaiming peace, announcing news of happiness,
 D A E   A A^7
Our God reigns, our God reigns.

    D   A
Our God reigns, our God reigns,
    D E   A
Our God reigns, our God reigns.

Leonard E. Smith, Jnr.
Copyright © 1974, 1978 Thankyou Music.

Step 3: Melody playing

Melody playing is a most attractive way of playing the guitar and for a nylon-strung guitar the main style it was designed for. It is worth trying to learn. Some people find it difficult and, in my experience, these are older people whose fingers are more stiff, those who have no musical knowledge at all or those who are very strong strummers. On the other hand teenagers, those who have enjoyed picking and naturally musical people have little problem. Try it, then treat it as an option if you really struggle.

First example: I love You, Lord, *first line of words as a melody*

The first task is to learn where these four notes are in music and on the guitar. You will immediately see that three of them are open strings.

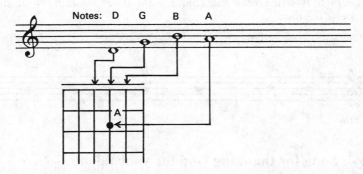

2. Do not go any further until you really know how to read these four notes in music and on the guitar. Test yourself thoroughly.
3. Here now is the first line of the music of *I love You, Lord. Never* write in the names of the notes because you will always then look at the names and never learn to read the notes. Read them over and over again out loud until you are fluent.

hold

Laurie Klein
Copyright © 1978, 1980 House of Mercy Music/
Maranatha! Music/Word Music UK.

Key:

o = open string

⌣ = tied note: don't play the 2nd one

2 = your 2nd left hand finger (middle)

71

4. Now play slowly. The numbers refer to your left hand fingers. The 'o' means an open string. You only have to 'make' one note and that is A in the last bar. Don't worry about reading the rhythm. You know the song and also have the tape to follow.
5. Finally learn how to use the right hand. You will get the best sound if you use your right index and middle fingers alternately. You use a *rest* stroke. This means you push the string gently with the pad of your finger and come to rest on the string below. So when you play the first note, open D string, with your index finger you will come to rest against the A string. Then you play the open G string, the 2nd note, with your middle finger, and come to rest against the open D string, and so on. It feels as though your fingers are walking.

Exercise for right hand playing style

On the high B string play the sound eight times, walking your fingers alternately like this:

Step 4: Song for thanking God for your talents—*Give thanks*

How to play

1. Use the capo on fret 3 as instructed, then you can use the chord in the key of D. Listen to the tape for an explanation of how to use a capo.
2. This will give you more practice with the chord of DM7.
3. Use the syncopated strum. Listen on the tape to how Roger plays the two bars where you have three chords, eg 'poor say I am rich'.

NB: This song is not easy for weak bar chord players. But now is the time to start improving your playing of bar chords and the next two sessions will concentrate on them.

GIVE THANKS

        D   A
Give thanks with a grateful heart

      Bm   F#m
Give thanks to the Holy One

```
        G                   D           C        Em-A⁷
Give thanks because He's given Jesus Christ His Son (Repeat)
```

```
    F#m         Bm        A Bm Em7
And now let the weak say 'I am strong'
```

```
            G A Dmaj7
Let the poor say 'I am rich'
```

```
    F#m      Bm              C      Em ⁷
Because of what the Lord has done for us.
```

```
    F#m         Bm       A Bm   Em⁷
And now let the weak say 'I am strong'
```

```
        A      G A Dmaj7
Let the poor say 'I am rich'
```

```
    F#m   Bm              C      Em7
Because of what the Lord has done for us.
```

```
            A⁷   D
Last time end—Give thanks
```

SESSION 14

Why Sing New Songs?

Step 1: Bible study

There is a special outpouring of new songs in this decade and it is helpful to stop and look at the biblical background to see both why we sing new songs and what their purpose is.

Read these three passages from the Psalms before you answer the questions: Psalm 33:3–4; 96:1–4; 98:1.

Questions

1. All of these verses start with a ....
   (promise/warning/command?). Surely this alone is sufficient reason for
   singing a new song—God tells us to.

2. Each of the same Psalms gives a reason for singing new songs. I have
   given you the first one. Complete the other two:

   Psalm 33:4   because God's word is true and he is faithful

   Psalm 96:4   ....

   Psalm 98:1   ....

Finally, from Ephesians 5:18–20 we have a clue as to why we are singing so
many new songs in the 1980s and 90s. If we are filled with the ....
.... we will praise God with all the rich variety of music—old Psalms,
the best of the hymns and songs inspired by the ....
Many Christian leaders tell us that God is pouring out the Holy Spirit in
many areas of the world in greater power and extent than at any other time
since Christ. No wonder the same Holy Spirit is inspiring a creativity of
response in his people.

Thought

Why not sit down now and just start singing to the Lord. You might sing an
old song with a new realisation of its meaning or find the Holy Spirit gives
you a brand new song.

Step 2: Bar chords with E major shape—F, F#, G, G# and A

Once you realise that the most common bar chords use only *four* main
shapes the problem of learning how to play them and where to find them
diminishes. In this session we will take the shape of the very first chord you
learned—that of E. Follow these stages of learning:

1. Look at the diagram carefully seeing the whole *shape*, then put your left
   hand fingers down *but* use fingers 2, 3 and 4. In other words, do not use
   your index finger because this is going to be used to form the bar as you
   move up.

2. Move the whole shape up one fret, at the same time placing your index finger at fret 1 to form the bar. Since you have not altered the shape, you will still have a major chord but it will be one musical sound higher, and one musical sound higher than E is F. F major bar chord is not easy to play, but do not spend time struggling with it at this stage. Sometimes, on a cheaper guitar, even advanced players have difficulty. It is the next chord, F# major, which we are going to concentrate on now.
3. Move the shape up again laying your index finger this time at fret 2. Since the musical sound after F is F#, this will be the chord of F#major and it is indicated as F#. Do not confuse it with F#m which is the minor version. It is easier to play than F since you are already depressing a shorter length of string.

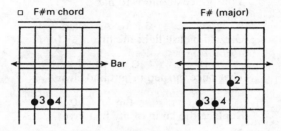

Step 3: Songs using F# bar chord

Song O Lord You're beautiful

This song is in *Songs of Fellowship*, but the chords of the key of D given in *Songifts* are better for this purpose of using F# as well as being a satisfactory key for singing.

How to play

Choose from the following possibilities according to your preference for strumming or picking. All styles need a gentle, smooth touch.

1. The basic ↓ ⌐⌐ strum with perfectly timed left hand changes.
2. The clock strum.
3. Picking style of T, i, $\frac{R}{m}$, i. If using this try another development when you have adjacent chords as in the G to D at the end of the first line. On each chord play the thumb then all three treble strings together, plucking them gently towards you. This variation is written like this:

Chord	G	D
Play	T $\frac{R}{m}$ i	T $\frac{R}{m}$ i
Rhythm	♫	♫

O Lord You're Beautiful

D   G D A
O Lord You're beautiful

D   G D A
Your face is all I see.

Bm   F#   Bm A D
For when Your eyes are on this child

G   D Asus4-A G-D
Your grace abounds to me.

G D A
O Lord please light the fire

D   G   D A
That once burned bright and clear.

Bm   F#   Bm A D
Replace the lamp of my first love

G   D Asus4-A G-D
That burns with holy fear.

Keith Green
Copyright © 1980 Birdwing Music/
Cherry Lane Music/Word Music (UK).

Song Whether you're one *by Graham Kendrick*

Whether You're One

E   F#
Whether you're one or whether you're two

A   E
or three or four or five.

F#
Six or seven or eight or nine,

A   E
It's good to be alive.

A6   E
It really does not matter how old you are,

```
     F#              B7sus4    B7
Jesus loves you whoever you are

   E        F#        A         E
La la la la-la la la la la, Jesus loves us all.
```

Graham Kendrick
Copyright © 1986 Thankyou Music.

How to play

1. This children's song can be played at fret 4 with the key of G chords but doing this means you still have to play the bar chord of F. It has an advantage of sounding brighter, but I recommend playing it without a capo in the key of E.
2. Line 5 may present some chord problems. A6 is drawn below (although you should by now be familiar with the method of working out these altered chords). The 6th note of A major scale is F#. Since our main new chord of F# this week is found at the 2nd fret I hope you quickly realise that the note F# will also be there. Here is a diagram of this chord.

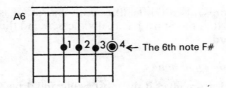

B7sus4 is both easy and important to use because the altered note is also in the melody of the song. The 4th note of B is E and since you have an open high string E just remove your 4th finger from the normal B7 chord so leaving the string free.

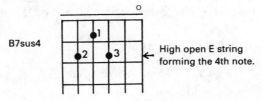

3. The best strum for the right hand is the syncopated.

Step 4: Location of G, G# and A major bar chords

Remember that we are dealing with the major chord shape of E this session. After F# at the 2nd fret the next three chords, ascending one fret at a time

77

retaining the shape, will give you the next three musical sounds. These are G, G# and A. Learn now the positions of all these five chords from the useful diagram below and play them daily this week until you know exactly where they are.

FRET	E major shape
1	F major
2	F# major
3	G major
4	G# major
5	A

Note: The *bar* chord versions of G and A are worth learning. They have a brighter sound and sometimes make easier reached alternatives to the basic forms.

Step 5: Song *Hosanna*

This praise song presents no difficulties with chords. It is one of the new songs of the 1980s that the Spirit has really blessed and throughout it exalts Jesus Christ as Lord.

How to play with the right hand

1. The syncopated strum gives it the most swing and drive, but be careful of bars with two chords when you change on the up swing. If you listen to the tape I think you will get it immediately without too much analysis.
2. The two bars of 'Lord we lift up Your Name' and 'with hearts full of praise' are good if you change the strum to ↓ ↑↓↑↓↓↑. This will emphasise the rhythm of these bars.
3. Finally, play three string single down strum chords on 'Lord my God' in the last line.

Now really enjoy it and exalt Jesus as Lord.

HOSANNA

```
    G         D       Em      C    D
Hosanna, Hosanna, Hosanna in the highest
```

```
    G         D       Em      C    D
Hosanna, Hosanna, Hosanna in the highest
```

```
  C         D             G
Lord we lift up Your Name
```

```
    C        D              G
With hearts full of praise

    C     D      G    D    Em
Be exalted O Lord my God

       C          D    G
Hosanna in the highest.
```

Carl Tuttle
Copyright © 1985 Mercy Publishing/
Thankyou Music.

SESSION 15

Choosing Songs for Christian Worship

Step 1: Bible study

A subject very close to my heart is the great need we all have to grow in love and tolerance towards each other's choice of Christian music. At the same time we all need to check that our choice

1. Is a response to a true biblical picture of God.
2. Is in line with the long tradition of Christian music whose roots go back to Jewish Old Testament times.

The passage that will best guide us is Ephesians 5:18–20. Read it carefully.

Question: Which members of the Trinity are mentioned? . . . .

Yes, all three because our God *is* trinitarian. We can easily lose the balance.

Practical exercise: Write down six pieces of Christian worship music that your fellowship is using a great deal at the moment:

. . . .

. . . .

. . . .

Put a capital G next to those that mention God.
Put a capital J next to those that mention Jesus.
Put capitals HS next to those that mention Holy Spirit.

Reflect and decide if you need to suggest a redress of balance. At the same time remember that the chief function of Holy Spirit is to glorify Jesus so there *are* fewer songs that mention him directly.

Question: Name the three types of music mentioned in Ephesians 5:19 that the New Testament church obviously used.

Answer: . . . .

Beware of thinking that only spiritual songs are inspired by the Spirit. This passage teaches otherwise, and if we are filled with the Spirit some of the great hymns of the church come alive in a most marvellous way. I regard Graham Kendrick's *Who can sound, Servant King* and *Meekness and Majesty* as examples of recent hymns.

Step 2: Bar chords that use the E minor shape—F, Gm, G#m and Am

The same method of learning as we used for the E major series applies to these.

1. Put down the Em chord but using your 3rd and 4th fingers.
2. Move the shape up one fret, at the same time placing the index finger down as a bar at fret 1. You now have Fm.
3. Move up again so that at fret 2 you have F#m, a chord you know.
4. Continue three more times and check with this location diagram. The most important chord to learn for this week's song is Gm at the 3rd fret.

FRET	E minor shape
1	Fm
2	F#m
3	Gm
4	G#m
5	Am

Step 3: Song *Jesus put this song into our hearts*

JESUS PUT THIS SONG INTO OUR HEARTS

Dm   A
Jesus put this song into our hearts

80

Dm

Jesus put this song into our hearts

D   Gm

It's a song of joy no one can take away

A   Dm

Jesus put this song—into our hearts.

Graham Kendrick
Copyright © 1986 Thankyou Music.

How to play

1. I suggest you do not use a capo—partly so that you can practise this Gm chord.
2. The right hand needs to use a developing strum as the music speeds up.
   (a) For the slow start with its lovely Hebrew flavour use *either* the pick/
   strum *or* with your fingers get a similar effect using the T m style.

$$\begin{array}{c} R \\ T\ m \\ i \end{array}$$

   (b) As the song speeds up you could develop the pick/strum in various ways. For instance:
   (i)   Double the 2nd down strum to Pick $\overset{1}{}\ \overset{2\ and}{\downarrow\uparrow}$.
   (ii) Make it even stronger by playing ⬇⬇ ⬇⬆ .
   This last strum, with its emphasis on down beats, helps to keep the people together. Apply these ideas to other Israeli-type songs.

Step 4: 3-beat strum and picking styles—song *Abba Father*

Strangely enough many people are not strong rhythmically in playing songs with only three beats.

Strum for 3-beat songs

In Session 3 I gave you the basic, steady 3-beat strum shown here as example 1. This can be altered by picking a single bass string for the first beat and often has the advantage of then shadowing the melodic flow.

Example 1.	1	2 and	3 and
	↓	↓↑	↓↑

Example 2.	1	2 and	3 and
	Pick	↓↑	↓↑

Finger picking style

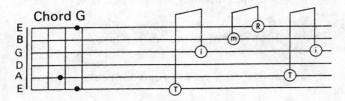

Chord G

Try this to the 3-beat song *Abba Father* and also go back to the song *Set my spirit free* which you learned in Session 4. Note that the thumb is used twice and must play the bass strings that match the chord you are playing.

ABBA FATHER

G	C	D	G

Abba Father let me be

	C	D	G

Yours and Yours alone.

	C	D	G

May my will for ever be

C	D	G

Evermore Your own.

B7	Em	B7		Em

Never let my heart grow cold

C	Am	D-D7

Never let me go.

G	C	D	G

Abba Father let me be

C	D	G

Yours and Yours alone.

Step 5: Melody playing using the notes C and D and the chorus of *Tell me why*

Each of these steps dealing with melody playing builds on what was taught before, so quickly revise what you learned in Step 3 of Session 13. If you really learn these next notes C and D you will have the satisfaction of being able to play all the chorus of *Tell me why*.

1. We learned the position of the note C when we worked out the chord of Gsus4. Look back to page 64. Fix it very clearly now in your mind both in relation to the musical staff and the guitar fretboard. The note D is two frets higher.
2. This song also needs the open string E which in music is written in the top space. So the whole chorus only uses these five notes. Two of them are open strings.

Here are the five notes written in music and on the fretboard:

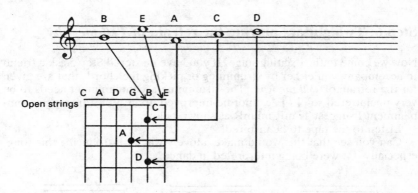

3. Next, learn to read the names of the notes. Do this *before* you try to play them. Remember—*don't* write down the names of the notes or you will never learn to read them.

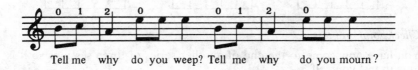

Tell me   why   do you weep? Tell me   why   do you mourn?

4. Next, play it thinking of the words so that you get the rhythm correct.
5. The next line 'Tell me why do you mourn' is exactly the same.
6. The 3rd line has just two more notes at the end, the C again and open B.

Tell me   why   do you look   so   sad?

7. You will be able to complete the verse by repeating the first phrase twice and then playing the last phrase with this ending.

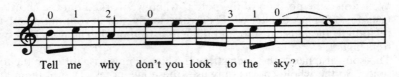

Tell me why don't you look to the sky? _____

Step 6: Two guitars playing the refrain of *Tell me why*

Now we come to the exciting stage. If you have mastered Step 5 ask a friend to accompany you either by strumming or picking the chords that are given for the refrain of *Tell me why*. The strumming accompaniment needs to be very uncluttered so ↓↓↑↑ cannot be improved upon. For a picking accompaniment I suggest Ti mR mi mR as shown below.

Listen to the tape to be inspired!

Can you see that this would make a lovely way of introducing this song, especially if it were being interpreted in dance.

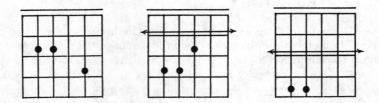

Checkpoint and test

You have now come to the end of another series of three sessions so it is time to test yourself.

1. Play these chords and name them:

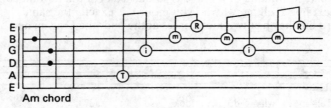

Am chord

(6 marks)

2. Name these notes:

(5 marks)

3. Play the song *Rejoice in the Lord always* in the key of E without using music. Be honest and give yourself 2 marks if you did it.　　(2 marks)
4. Use your guitar to help to complete the positions of these bar chords:

F# is found at fret no. . . . . using the . . . . chord shape.

Gm is found at fret no. . . . . using the . . . . chord shape.
5. Ephesians gives us the three main styles of New Testament music:

'Speak to one another in . . . ., ... and . . . .'

(3 marks)

SESSION 16

The Changed Heart

Step 1: Bible study—the spiritual limitation of music

You might be surprised at the implication in the title of this study, but I believe that we musicians need to be aware that music itself will not convert a person. Celebration must always include proclamation. We lead people in praise and singing to prepare the way for God's word and Holy Spirit. Support for this teaching comes in the well-known story of David playing his harp in King Saul's service.

Read: 1 Samuel 16:14–23. The background to this story is that Saul has disobeyed God—he was already going the 'wrong way'. It has been suggested that he suffered from some form of mental illness. The Old Testament explains this with the phrase 'an evil spirit tormented him'. For our purpose, concentrate on the following three questions.

Questions

1. What solution did Saul's servants suggest for his tormented mind?

. . . .

2. In verse 23 what is the key word that gives away the fact that Saul was not deeply changed, 'he only .... better'?

3. From chapter 18, verses 6–11 what happened the next time David played to Saul? ....

So music will not cure a jealous spirit, convert a non-believer or fully heal mental sickness, though it does help tremendously by opening up a person to God's Spirit.

What then is the cure? Read the promise in Ezekiel 36:26. God says: 'I will give you a .... and put a new .... in you.' This promise becomes true as a person accepts Jesus Christ as Saviour and Lord. He or she then has a new heart and is a new creation.

Positive application for you

Rejoice in the realisation that in using your guitar in worship you will help people to feel better and so prepare them to receive the word of God and the Spirit. What a responsibility, but what a joy and privilege.

Step 2: Chords with the Am shape—B♭m, Bm, Cm, C#m, Dm

Look first of all at the above list of chords that this bar chord shape enables you to play. In particular note:

1. Bm is certainly the most common and you have already come across it. Now is the time to perfect it.
2. C#m is the full version of the chord we learned in Session 12. Not only is it a good sounding chord, but it often occurs in songs that use G#m, the chord you learned last session. Both are played at fret 4. Remember this.
3. Dm played as a bar chord at fret 5 has a good full sound. You will remember from Session 7 that the root position version only uses four strings.

How to learn and play these bar chords

Follow exactly the same procedure you learned for the E and Em bar chord shapes.

1. Put down the Am chord using fingers 2, 3 and 4.
2. Move the whole shape up one fret, at the same time placing the 1st (index) finger as a bar at fret 1. You now have the chord of B♭m because B♭ is the next highest musical sound after A. It can also be called A#, but you will rarely meet this in guitar songs.

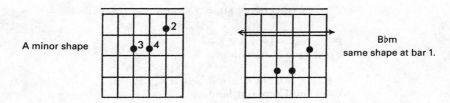

A minor shape

Bbm
same shape at bar 1.

3. Continue moving the shape and bar finger up a fret at a time and you will form the following series of chords. Learn at which fret they each come.

FRET	CHORD
1	Bbm
2	Bm
3	Cm
4	C#m
5	Dm

All based on Am shape.

4. At this stage start to root these minor bar chord positions in your fingers and mind by playing two chords at each fret, the first time with the Em shape and the second time with the Am shape. The most common ones to learn are those at frets 2 and 4:
   (a) At fret 2 play F#m and changing to Am shape play Bm (the most common pair).
   (b) At fret 4 play G#m and changing to Am shape play C#m.
   Make sure that you keep the bar index finger down as you change the shape. I hope this will convince you that the clarity of sound in bar chords comes from clean, firm changes of the fingers that make the shape.

Step 3: Song using minor chords at fret 4—*Lord have mercy on us* by Graham Kendrick

This song is chosen for two reasons:

1. It will give you technical practice with G#m and C#m bar chords. The Cdim chord is taught in Session 19, but you can omit it.
2. It relates to the Bible study in that the song speaks of the need we have *corporately* to seek the Lord's mercy and cleansing for a new heart.

E   G#m   A-B⁷
Lord have mercy on us,

 E   G#m   A-B⁷
Come and heal our land,

 C#m   B⁷
Cleanse with Your fire,

Cdim   C#m
Heal with Your touch

Amaj⁷   G#m   F#m   B⁷
Humbly we bow and call upon You now

  C   D   E
O Lord, have mercy on us.

  C   D   E
O Lord, have mercy on us.

How to play

1. Be most conscious of the sound and richness of each chord. They are beautifully chosen to enhance the depth of feeling in this song. Your fingers are but an extension of your heart.
2. Try the A major chord in bar 3 at fret 5 with the E major shape. It helps to lift the prayer towards God.
3. *Strum:* This needs to be uncluttered and clear because the chords are the chief vehicle of the musical message. I suggest the syncopated strum in a strong, controlled way. Build up in volume as you reach that magical change to C major on 'O Lord, have mercy on us'.

Step 4: Song/prayer: *Change my heart, O God* by Eddie Espinosa; new chord CM7

This song is a prayer for the ongoing change we all need of our hearts towards God's will. Technically it is easy but does give you the opportunity to learn a new chord, a new picking style and the triplet strum.

CM7   Dm-G   C-CM7
Change my heart, O God, make it ever true

       Dm-G   C-E7
Change my heart, O God, may I be like You

    Am Dm G7 C-E7
You are the potter, I am the clay

      Am   D D7 G— CM7
Mould me and make me, this is what I pray.

       Dm-G   C-CM7
Change my heart, O God, make it ever true

       Dm-G   C
Change my heart, O God, may I be like You.

Eddie Espinosa
Copyright © 1982 Mercy Publishing/Thankyou Music.

Chord CM7

After learning all those bar chords you will be glad to know that this is easy and effective. First of all, do you remember from Session 11 how to work out these major 7th chords? If not, take a minute to look back to page 58 so that you are always building on material learned previously. Now go on:

1. Look at the major scale of C drawn here. Note that it has no sharps or flats.

2. The 7th note is B.
3. On the guitar this is the open B string.
4. To play this chord therefore simply think of playing the normal C chord omitting the index finger. It will look like this:

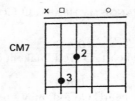

CM7

New picking style for this song

An attractive style for this song is one that weaves a pattern on the three treble strings of G, B and E. The thumb will always play the bass string appropriate to the chord. This pattern below emphasises the index finger and brings out the highest note of each chord at a good place.

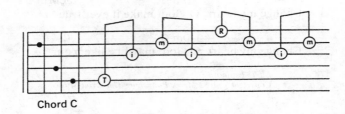

Chord C

Playing triplets and changing to a strum

When the song reaches the words 'You are the potter' you will note that the musical notes are written like this ♪♪♩ . This is called a *triplet* in music and means that three notes are to be played in the same time usually taken by two.

  Because it comes on words that link the prayer with the description of God, emphasise the triplet by playing three firm steady *down* strums like this:

  After the triplet I suggest that you move into a strum. I deliberately suggest this common, steady 4-beat strum rather than the syncopated because it is nearest in rhythm to the picking style you have just used.

↓ ↓↑↑↓↓↑

Song Within the veil

This song will give you more practice with the new chord of CM7 and it relates to the Bible study beautifully. Once we have a new heart and acknowledge Jesus Christ as Saviour we can come within the veil into the very presence of God (see Hebrews 10:19–20).

Ruth Dryden
Copyright © 1978 Genesis Music/Thankyou Music.

SESSION 17

Alone with God

Step 1: Bible study

This Bible study follows on from the one in Session 16 where we looked at the need for a changed heart. This ongoing transformation of the heart needs time and space spent alone with God. Spend a few minutes working through this study in the presence of God before you pick up your guitar again.

Read: Exodus 24:12–18 and Psalm 63:1,6.

Questions

1. Which two great Old Testament figures spent time alone with God?

    .... and ....

2. Write down three of the places mentioned for these encounters.

    ....

    The first two geographical areas may be difficult for us to reach regularly, but we all go the third place every night!

3. From Exodus 24:16 what did Moses receive during his time with God?

    ....

    For us the equivalent would be a word from Scripture or 'heard' in our heart.

4. From Psalm 63:7 what did David's time alone lead him to do?

    ....

Finally, read Mark 1:35 and Matthew 6:6 and complete the following sentence to discover Jesus' attitude to time spent alone with God:

Jesus believed in time spent alone because he himself ....

and also .... [commands/advises/suggests] us to do the same.

Meditation

Before you carry on with Step 2 of this session, decide prayerfully before God which time of day *tomorrow* you will spend with him alone.

Step 2: New picking style and strum for a new song, *I exalt Your Holy Name, O Lord*

Here is a lovely worship song to use in your time alone with God. You can accompany it with the 3-beat strum given in Session 16 or try a new pattern of finger picking with three beats. It is subtly different from the one given in Session 10, not only because it only has three beats but also because it brings out the middle finger.

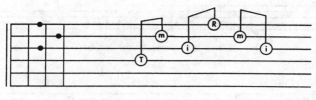

Chord D

Practise it using the chord progression given in the first line of the song. If you listen critically to your picking style for the last two chords you will hear how the middle finger emphasises the fall of the 4th note of A4 onto the normal 3rd note of the A chord.

The only way to learn picking skilfully is to practise as slowly as I demonstrate on the tape.

I EXALT YOUR HOLY NAME, O LORD

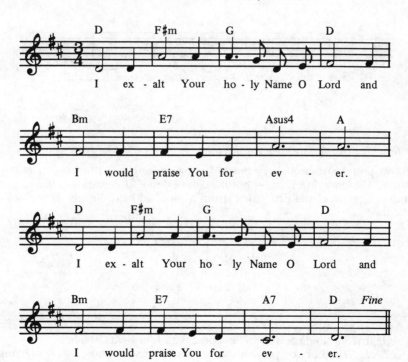

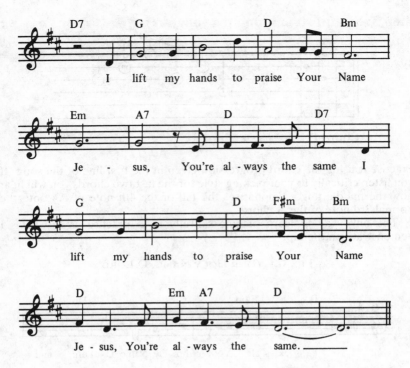

D7   G   D   Bm

I lift my hands to praise Your Name

Em   A7   D   D7

Je - sus, You're al - ways the same I

G   D   F♯m   Bm

lift my hands to praise Your Name

D   Em   A7   D

Je - sus, You're al - ways the same. _____

Words and music by Carl Smith.
Reproduced by permission.

Alternative strumming style for the song

If you prefer strumming try the following variation of the basic ↓ ♫ ♫ strum. The only difference—but it makes *all* the difference—is the accent and elongation of the first down strum of the 2nd beat. So the strum looks like this:

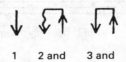

1   2 and   3 and

You learned a similar effect in Session 2 with four beats in a bar.

Check! Whether you play this song picking or strumming, are you being careful to sound the correct *bass* string for the beginning of every chord, eg the D string for D major and the A string for Bm?

Step 3: Skilful strumming for song *Majesty*

Being alone with God may lead us to have a richer revelation of his kingship, as Isaiah did in the temple in Jerusalem, or Peter on the Mount of Transfiguration. When this happens the well-known song *Majesty* is the perfect vehicle for a worship response of acclamation.

MAJESTY

G   C—— Am7
Majesty, worship His majesty,

          G   Em A7   Am— D7
Unto Jesus be glory, honour and praise.

   G   C—Am7
Majesty, kingdom authority

   D7   G   D7
Flow from His throne unto His own,

            G-C-G
His anthem raise.

   D7   G
So exalt, lift up on high the Name of Jesus

       D7   B7—D7
Magnify, come glorify Christ Jesus the King

G   C—— Am7
Majesty, worship His majesty,

   D7   G   D7
Jesus who died now glorified,

         G-C-G
King of all kings.

Suggestion for playing Majesty

The power and dignity of the song requires a strong steady style. Very little new needs to be learned, but more skill is required.

1. Use the strong ↓↓⌐↓↓⌐↓↑ style from Session 8 as the basic strum.
    As in the 3-beat version mentioned above really *elongate* and *accentuate* that second beat. It should sound dominant in the whole strum.
2. You will notice that there are many examples of triplets in the music. If the guitar only starts shadowing them in the second half of the song 'so exalt, lift up on high...' the effect will be to lead people into greater volume and praise. For these triplets try using the following direction of strum because it brings you smoothly back onto a down strum for the next whole beat. The diagram illustrates it:

Words: 'lift up on'

Step 4: New major 7th chord and song *In His time*

This song has been chosen because it would make a good final song in your times alone with the Lord. If you try it with the following chords it will enable you to use another easy but lovely major 7th chord, FM7.

FM7
Here is the scale of F major:

This 7th note of E is your high open E string so the chord is the same as the 3-string easy F major version *plus* that open E string.

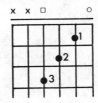

How to play the song

1. An effective way to start this song (and an idea that can be used in many slower songs) is to play the first two notes of the melody as you sing them, moving into a strum or pick on the third word 'time'. The two melody notes are middle C and E, that is, lower sounding notes than we have met so far. Here they are in music and on the guitar fretboard.

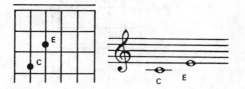

2. Strum the rest of the song with a gentle syncopation, but pick the first beat of every bar. Doing this really brings out the colours of the chord changes. Listen to the tape as Robbie and I demonstrate this.

IN HIS TIME

Diane Ball
Copyright © 1978 Maranatha Music USA/Word Music UK.

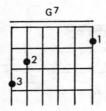

G⁷

Step 5: Melody playing of all the song *In His time* (optional extra)

This is not difficult to play. I have written it an octave higher for the purpose of melody playing. Doing this, as with the other melodies you are learning, enables it to be accompanied nicely by a second guitar strumming. There is only one new note for you to learn and that is the high note of A on the E string. You already know where G is (at the 3rd fret), so allowing for G# this note of A will be at the 5th fret. This should link in your mind with the bar chord versions of A and Am (also at fret 5).

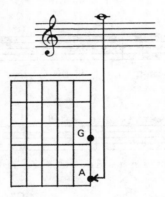

Before you start to learn the whole song, practise moving onto this high note of A correctly. You must *slide* the left hand 3rd finger you use for G up two frets to reach A. Learn this phrase first, then you will have no difficulty with the rest of the song. Be careful to follow my left hand fingering exactly.

Right hand fingers

Meeting God at the Cross

Step 1: Bible study—the shape of the cross

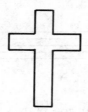

The very shape of the cross with its intersection of the vertical and horizontal reminds us that in all *our* search for God this is the place where *he* has chosen to meet us.

Read: 2 Corinthians 5:17–21.

Questions

1. Complete this sentence from verse 19: 'God was .... the

   world to himself in ....'

2. Which two men were drawn to God through the cross even before Christ was taken down from it?

   (a) .... (Luke 23:40–43).

   (b) .... (Mark 15:39).

3. How does this affect us as we learn to play the guitar in order to lead others to worship God more meaningfully?

   (a) Take Paul as a model, who, for all his intellect said, 'I resolved to know nothing while I was with you except ....

   ....' (1 Corinthians 2:2).

   (b) List three or four songs that your church or fellowship sing whose words or meaning focus on the cross.

   ....

   ....

   If you struggled to think of any, this week's session will equip you

99

with two more: *I met You at the cross* by Roger Jones and *The Servant King* by Graham Kendrick.

Step 2: New chord E6

In Session 11 you learned the altered chord that uses the 4th note of the scale of E—the chord of E4. Now we need the 6th note of that scale:

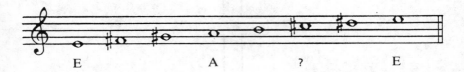

Complete the sentence: The 6th note of the scale of E is .... and it is found at the .... fret on the open .... string.

How to play the E6 chord clearly

E6 is one of those chords that require adding a finger to the existing chord and stressing the new note. Look at the diagram and play each string separately until you are satisfied with the clear sound under your little finger that is making C#.

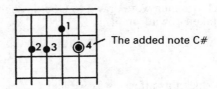

The added note C#

Next, look at the word this chord accompanies in the first line of every verse. Yes...it is the word 'cross', the whole point of the song and this week's session.

I MET YOU AT THE CROSS

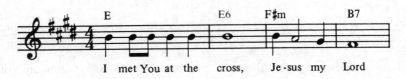

I met You at the cross, Je-sus my Lord

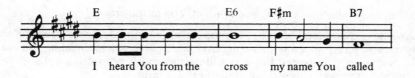

I heard You from the cross my name You called

Asked me to fol-low You all of my days

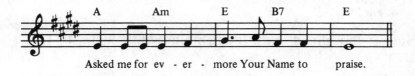

Asked me for ev - er - more Your Name to praise.

Step 3: New strum for playing this week's songs

So far you have learned to alter a basic strum either by doubling one of the beats or stressing a beat by elongating the strum. This strum takes you a stage further by teaching you to subdivide a basic beat into four. In music and strum patterns you will then have this development:

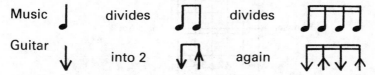

Any beat can be subdivided but for this week's songs I suggest the 2nd beat. This will make the complete strum look like this:

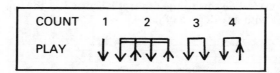

When to use this new strum in song I met You at the cross

As I have mentioned before, the purpose of learning different strums is to be able to interpret songs meaningfully. The people you are leading will *not* be analysing your strums, but they will unconsciously respond to a change of strum. In this way you will facilitate their worship.

In this week's first song bring the new strum in only during the last verse. A suggested progression would be:

1. For the first two lines of verse 1 use the basic ↓ ↓↑ strum.
2. As you reach the words 'asked me to follow You' develop it to ↓ ↓↑↓↑ ↓↑ .
3. For either the whole of verse 3 or for the last two lines use the new development. This is suggested because it is only in verse 3 that we sing a response to Christ's question of whether we will follow him all the days of our lives.

Step 4: Bar chords with the A major shape—B♭, B, C, C#, D, E♭

This series is the fourth and last of the major groups of chord shapes needed for bar chords that you are likely to meet. In Session 10 we learned the progression based on the Am shape. Now it is those based on A major. Work through the steps one at a time as you have done before.

1. Put down the A major shape at fret 2 but using the 2nd, 3rd and 4th fingers. Play this basic A chord.
2. Move the shape up to fret 3, at the same time laying your index bar finger at fret 1. Be sure that you have an empty space at fret 2. This chord is one musical sound higher than A, ie B♭ (rarely called by its other name of A# in guitar music).

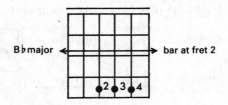

3. Carry on moving the shape up to the 6th fret. You will then have this series. I have taken this to the 6th fret because it is the only position for playing E♭ with any degree of ease!

Fret	A major shape
1	B♭
2	B
3	C
4	C#
5	D
6	E♭

Two points to notice about this series:

1. The chords of B♭ and E♭ must be known, but they come in keys that are not best suited to the dynamics of the guitar. It is perhaps helpful to realise that all instruments have their stronger and weaker keys—ask any flautist or clarinet player. If a complete song is in the key of B♭ or E♭ the guitarist will often be advised to use a capo, but more often you will meet these chords as occasional ones with another key. This is the case with this week's second song, *The Servant King*.
2. You might wonder why it is necessary to learn the chords of C and D as bar chords. As bar chords they are played higher up the fretboard and quite a different effect is achieved. The whole sound is brighter. Sometimes also it is easier to move to a bar chord version than revert to the root position.

Song The Servant King *by Graham Kendrick*

How to play

1. With the capo at fret 3 and using the chords printed keep a steady basic strum for the verse: ↓ ♫♫♫ .
2. At the point of changing to the refrain change to the strum written here below. You will realise that it is a further development of the subdivision of a beat into four which you learned in Step 3.

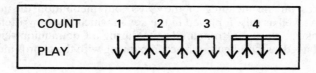

3. Verses 2 or 3 are beautiful sung by a solo voice and accompanied with picking.
4. Note that there is a B major chord three bars from the end, so refer to the chart in Step 4 to see where it is found.

Capo 3 (Cm)   Am   E   FM^7-G
            From heaven You came, helpless babe,

                      C   F—G—G
            Enter'd our world, Your glory veiled,

      Am   E   FM7-G
            Not to be served but to serve,

                  C   F   C   G
            And give Your life that we might live.

Refrain

                C-G   Am-Am^7
*   This is our God, the Servant King,*

              F   G   C-G
*   He calls us now to follow Him*

                C   C^7 C-B
*   To bring our lives as a daily offering*

                C   G   C
*   Of worship to the Servant King.*

Step 5: Melody playing of hymn *Glory be to Jesus* (optional extra)

This melody is chosen for two reasons. Most important, the words of the hymn focus on the meaning of the cross, our meditation theme for this session. As well as this, if played in the key in which I have written it below it also makes a lovely instrumental song during a Communion service. For this it will need a second guitarist accompanying with the chords indicated in circles.

How to play

1. The whole hymn only uses six notes. Two of them are the open strings B and E. You have already learned the other four, but here they are all together for quick reference.

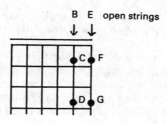

B E open strings

2. Read the musical names of the notes first.
3. Before you play the first two open E notes place the left hand finger ready for the third note of D, that is, on the 3rd fret of the B string.
4. Remember to alternate the right hand index and middle fingers.

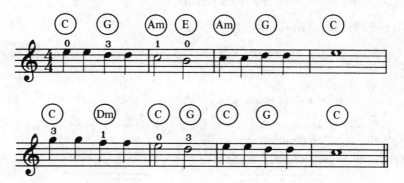

Traditional

SESSION 19

'Do Not Lose Heart'

Step 1

! STOP !
! CHECK !
! PRAY !

Questions

1. Are you keeping up with the course?
2. Have you—like me—too many books and manuals that you never quite finished?

Many of you, I am sure, are quietly smiling. We are all so human and it is not easy to keep going to the end, especially if you are learning on your own.

But let me encourage you...the worst is over!

The last three sessions might sound difficult with names such as 'augmented', 'diminished', etc, but in actual fact these chords are much easier than bar chords. In fact they are fairly rare chords, but they do add just that last bit of flavour to our music and make it extra beautiful for God.

Word of encouragement

Be like Paul and say, 'Therefore, since through God's mercy we have this ministry we do not lose heart' (2 Corinthians 4:1). Do you remember receiving the same exhortation in Session 5? Are you not encouraged to realise how far you have come since then?

Step 2: Diminished chords

Let your spirit rise even more as you read three simple facts about diminished chords.

1. They all have the same shape.
2. Each position of the shape gives a choice of four diminished chords at once.
3. You only need to move the shape up as high as fret 3 in order to learn all twelve possible diminished chords.

Here is the shape at fret 1:

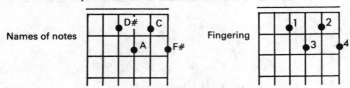

This position of the shape will give you the four diminished chords of the four notes on the diagram, that is, D#dim, Adim, Cdim and F#dim. We will meet C and F#dim in songs in this course.

For your future reference here are the other two positions of the shape with the names of the notes that are the basis of the respective chords.

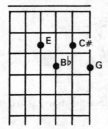
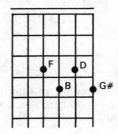

What does 'diminished' mean?

Simply that the distance between the notes of the chord is diminished or made smaller. So whereas a major chord of C would have C to E to G, a diminished has C to E♭ to G♭.

C major   C diminished

Step 3: Song with diminished chord — *Such love*

How to play

1. Use the chords given. This will then use the F#dim chord.
2. Try the capo at fret 3. This gives a good pitch for leading a small group. Note however that if you are playing with a keyboard player who is using the music as written, you must use the capo at fret 4.
3. The triplets are again important and I recommend you use the three down strokes you learned in Session 16.
4. For the rest of the song use a strum that will enable you to interpret it from your own heart.

SUCH LOVE

Capo at fret 3   C-Am   Dm   G
Such love, pure as the whitest snow,

                Dm-G   F   C-Esus4
Such love, weeps for the shame I know,

            E   Am   Fmaj7   F#dim
Such love, paying the debt I owe

         C-Fmaj7 G   C
O Jesus, such love.

Graham Kendrick
Copyright © 1988 Make Way Music.

Step 4: Song for Christmas — *Silent Night*

Since this song was originally composed for a guitar one Christmas Eve in Austria it is a little gem to play. In the midst of all the learning of rarer chords just sit back and enjoy playing this.

Picking style

When you have a song with such a lovely simple melody keep the guitar accompaniment uncluttered. So the very basic 3-beat picking style is ideal. You learned it in Session 6.

But if you listen to the tape you will hear how the bass can be brought out to shadow the melodic line. If you would like to try this, look at the way I have written the song below. The chords in brackets indicate the *bass* string to be picked. So for the first chord of A you pick the D string and this will give you the note E which is the first note of the melody. As you grasp this idea you will be able to apply it to other songs.

Silent Night

A(D)   A(A)   A(D)   A(A)
Silent night, Holy night.

E(A)   E⁷(D) A(A)   A(D)
All is calm, all is bright.

D(D)   A(D)   A(A)
Round yon virgin, mother and child,

D(D)   A(D)   A(A)
Holy infant, so gentle and mild.

E(A)   E7(D)   A(A)
Sleep in heavenly peace,

A(A)   E7(E)   A(A)
Sleep in heavenly peace.

Traditional
Franz Gruber (1787–1863)
Joseph Mohr (1792–1848)

Step 5: Melody and picking style for *Father we adore You*

This is an easy melody to play for it only has two notes that you have not met before. You have however met them in chord formation. They are C# and F#. Both of them are at the 2nd fret of the B and E strings respectively.

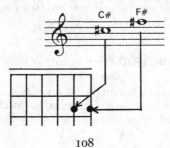

As you learn the song remember to follow the basic stages. One reason for failure—then frustration—is trying to go too quickly. So:

1. Read the musical notes of each phrase first. Learning to read music is just like learning to read a language as a five year old does. The more you practise aloud, the quicker your reading speed will be.
2. Only then pick up the guitar and play the first short phrase. A phrase is a musical sentence that follows the meaning of the words. So this song has three short phrases following the three lines of words.

FATHER WE ADORE YOU

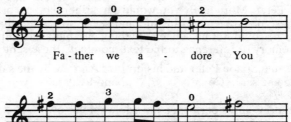

Fa - ther   we   a - dore   You

Lay   our   lives   be - fore   You

How   we   love   You.

New picking style

By now you will have realised that there are many permutations of a few basic styles. Gradually your fingers will start to weave their own patterns following the shape of the tune. Here is one idea:

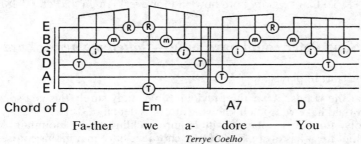

Chord of D   Em   A7   D

Fa-ther   we   a-   dore ———— You

Terrye Coelho
Copyright © 1972 Maranatha! Music/Word Music (UK).

109

Be a Peter

Step 1: Bible study—Peter the worshipper

You would probably not readily match the description of 'worshipper' with the apostle Peter. More likely you would say 'fisherman' or 'preacher'. But consider these peak events in his life and see if you agree that after such experiences he could not have been anything else but a worshipper.

From memory or reference to the texts complete these sentences:

1. As Jesus met Simon Peter and his brother Andrew by the side of the Sea of Galilee he said, 'Come .... and I will make you ....' (Mark 1:17).
2. Peter first saw Jesus perform a miracle when his own .... was healed (Mark 1:30–31).
3. When Jesus asked the diagnostic question, 'Who do you say I am?' Peter was the one who answered, 'You ....' (Mark 8:29).
4. Six days later Peter was one of the three disciples who saw Jesus ...... on the mountain (Mark 9:2).
5. While Jesus was being beaten and mocked, Peter ..... him and said to the people warming themselves at the fire ' ....' (Mark 14:71).
6. After his resurrection Jesus asked Peter three times, '..............?' (John 21:15).
7. Jesus' last command to Peter was, ' ....' (John 21:22).

How many of these kinds of experiences can you identify with? What clue do we have then that all these experiences made Peter a worshipper?

Read: 2 Peter 1:16–18. This letter of Peter, reflecting his experiences and beliefs, even if not perhaps written specifically by him, shows what memory stood out. Finally, what is Peter's last command to us—to you? 'Grow in .... To him be glory both now and for ever! Amen' (2 Peter 3:18).

Step 2: Song Peter could have sung—*Soften my heart, Lord*

Before you start to play:

1. Look at the words. After the previous Bible study surely this is a song Peter would have welcomed knowing after his denial of Christ.
2. Secondly, for you to play it will require tackling a last mountain of difficulties for it has every kind of new chord we have met in this course. But be a Peter—be determined to master the technical difficulties and

allow the Holy Spirit to equip you.

This second step, then, is written just to give you time to reflect, and redirect your will and prayer.

Step 3: Augmented chords

You will probably not meet these even as often as diminished chords. Just as diminished means making the interval between notes smaller, with augmented chords the interval is made bigger. All that happens is that the 5th note of the scale is raised a semitone.

Example: the major chord of C, E and G becomes C, E and G#.

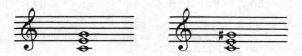

What is the shape of augmented chords?

A root position version can be used for B, E♭ and G.

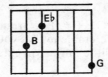

After this there is a shape that does not change, and once you have reached fret 4 you will have covered all the ones you need. Here is the series for reference:

Fingering

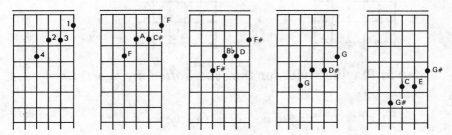

III

Step 4: Other chords needed for this song—Cdim, B♭maj7 and GM7

Cdim

See if you can play this chord without looking back to the last session when this was taught. When you pick this chord try to sound the note C first using your right hand middle finger. This will bring out the colour of the C diminished.

B♭maj7

I will help you to work this out. The 7th note of B♭ is A and you will remember that the note A is at fret 2 on the G string. So rearrange the normal B♭ bar chord to include this A and the chord will look like this:

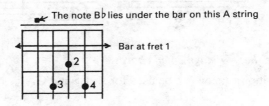

GM7

The 7th note of the scale of G is F#. Two arrangements of this chord can be tried—the second one is preferable in that you *can* play a 3-string version. With practice however the little finger will extend to make the correct bass of G to the chord.

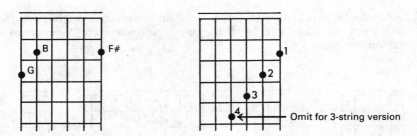

Step 5: Playing styles for the song *Soften my heart, Lord*

SOFTEN MY HEART, LORD

```
D          Em  Baug-Em7 A G   A    D-Dmaj7-D6
```
Soften my heart, Lord, sof-ten my heart.

D　　　　　Em　Baug-Em⁷ A　　　D-F#-Cdim
From all in-dif-ference—set me a-part.

　　　　　　　　Gmaj7 -A
To feel Your com-pas-sion

　　　　　　　F#m-Bm
To weep with Your tears.

　　　　B♭maj⁷　　　D F#m Bm
Come sof-ten my heart, O Lord.

B♭maj ⁷　　　D-Dsus4-D
Sof-ten my heart.

Graham Kendrick
Copyright © 1988 Make Way Music.

Now that you at least know *how* to play all the chords needed we can look at the possible playing styles. Below I have suggested three alternatives and all are demonstrated on the tape so you can decide which you like or which you would like to master. The first two are easy.

1. The basic 3-beat strum: ↓ ↓↑ ↓↑

2. A picking style that stresses the ring finger twice in each sequence:

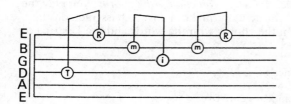

Remember to use the thumb on the bass string that matches the chord.

3. Picking so as to bring out the altered notes or notes of the melody. This is not easy to explain on paper, but if you read slowly, listen to each stage on the tape and imitate, you will succeed and add another skill to your playing.
   (a) In bar 1 where you have the words 'Soften my' the melody notes are F#, E and F# again. The position of these notes as you should now know is the 2nd fret of the high E string for the F# and the open string. So make sure your ring finger plays this string three times, but lift it off the string to make the open E. At the same time play the open D string to give the bar a chord basis. The index finger fills in the sound in between on the G string.

Tablature is a system of writing melody playing that you might meet. What I have described above, and what is demonstrated on the tape can be written in picture form of tablature. The six strings are represented by the six lines and the numbers refer to the *fret* to be played:

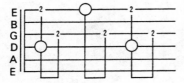

The figure 2 means depress the 2nd frets of the G and E strings with your left hand.

A similar playing style can be used in bar 5 where you have the words 'soften my' for the second time but using the melody notes E, D and E again. That phrase would look like this in tablature:

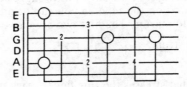

(b) A much simpler thing to do comes in line 2 when you have the words 'from all indifference'. If, *while you change the chords*, you play the bass string D you will actually make a lovely bass melodic line. Below I have written the chords with the words and the D string to be played each time.

From all in-diff-erence ─────

D(D)   Em(D) Baug(D)→Em7(D)

Step 6: Song *Father we love You*

This is a much easier song to finish with, but I chose it because it is also one Peter could have sung with joy once he had experienced God as trinitarian—Father, Son and Holy Spirit.

How to play

Start each verse quite gently with the simple key strum as given in Session 3. Remember that this keeps a group of people steadily together. But as you reach the long note halfway through each verse on 'earth' the song lifts in mood, so reflect this with your playing by developing the second beat into the quadruple division.

FATHER WE LOVE YOU

```
C           Dm              G7              C
Father we love You, we worship and adore You,

   Em           F            G-G7
Glorify Your name in all the earth.

   C           F        E7            Am
Glorify Your name, glorify Your name

   F           G7           C-G7-C
Glorify Your name in all the earth.
```

Donna Adkins
Copyright © 1976, 1981 Maranatha! Music/
Word Music (UK).

SESSION 21

The Destination of Worship

Step 1: Bible study

I believe that when we are asked to play our guitars to lead worship we must be quite clear where our destination is. It is no good leading people unless we ourselves know how to get there. I suggest there are two destinations:

First, our destination is the very presence of Almighty God.

Read: Revelation 4:1. As John looked through the door that for him opened into heaven he heard a voice inviting him to 'come up here'. In the rest of the chapter we read what a marvellous vision he had as he was taken into the presence of God.

Application for us

We need to spend time alone in God's presence before we can point others to that open door into his presence.

Where then is the second destination?

Read: Isaiah 6:1–8 (especially verse 8). After Isaiah had experienced the presence and cleansing of God, what question did he hear? 'I heard the voice of the Lord saying, " . . . . ?" '

What did Isaiah answer? ' . . . . '

The second destination of worship then is to tell others about Christ.

New Testament confirmation of these truths

It is always exciting to discover a clear teaching of Jesus that underlines principles laid down in the Old Testament. The Great Commission in Matthew 28 to go out and preach the gospel is well-known, but many people do not see what happened just before Jesus' command. Read verse 17 and write down what the disciples *did* when they met with the risen Christ on the mountain. 'When they saw him they . . . . '

So here again we have the two destinations: God's presence and the world.

If you are among those who do not doubt the presence of the risen Christ, you belong to Christ's body on earth and we must still go from our worship into his world to serve him there. This is worship in daily action.

Step 2: Three picking styles and song *Isn't He beautiful?*

The chords for this song present no problems and for this reason you might like to use it as a basis for learning three final styles of picking. There *are* other patterns, but this will complete the series that I have found useful. Note the emphasis of each one. After that the final choice is yours.

(a) Emphasises the index finger.

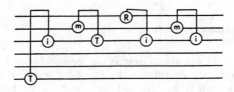

(b) Emphasises the thumb.

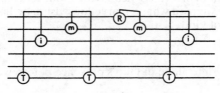

(c) A strong sound leading to a softer one.

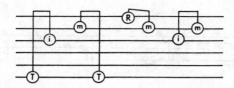

Step 3: Melody playing of *Isn't He beautiful?* (new note, high B)

This melody adds just one more note to your repertoire. In Session 17 you learned the position of the high note A on the E string. The note B is just two frets higher at fret 7.

The principle of moving onto it is the same. You will slide up the frets on the finger you use for the note before. If you start the whole of this phrase 'mighty God' in the third position, ie with the right index finger at fret 3 on the note G you can move smoothly. Here is the whole phrase written out with the left hand fingering. Try it and see how easy it is.

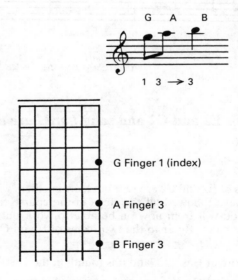

Here now is the notation of the whole song. Your left hand fingering is given and also the chord symbols for the second guitar to accompany.

John Wimber
Copyright © 1980 Mercy Publishing/Thankyou Music.

Step 4: Chords E2 and C2 and song *Lord have mercy on this nation*

New chords

These two chords of E2 and C2 are rare but learning them will enable you to see that if you have followed all the steps in the course that have taught chord building you will from now on be able to work out any other new chords you might meet. Refer to the two scales of E and C (pages 126 and 127 respectively).

1. The second note of E is . . . . and it is found on the D string at fret . . . . .

2. The second note of C is . . . . . . and it is found at the . . . . . . fret on the open B string.

These are the positions of the altered notes needed for these chords in this song.

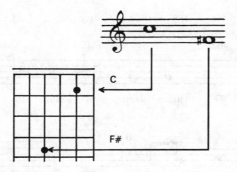

The final shape of the E2 and C2 chords therefore is:

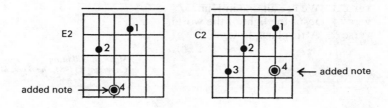

Song Lord have mercy on this nation

This song turns a worshipping group away from just concentrating on their own sin to seeing the corporate sin of a nation and pleading for the Lord's mercy. Listen to the tape then develop your own strum.

Step 5: *We are the children of God*

This is a good song, easy to play, and underlines the fact that we are Christ's body, witnessing in the world.

WE ARE THE CHILDREN OF GOD

We are the chil - dren of God.

We are the chil - dren of God.

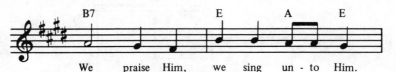

We praise Him, we sing un - to Him.

We are the chil - dren of God.

verse 2   We are the body of Christ.
verse 3   We are all one in Him.
verse 4   Jesus the light of the world.
verse 5   Africa back to God.

Maureen Wilkinson
Copyright © 1984 Thankyou Music.

Reference Section

Summary 1

I confess that I do not often read or use a reference section, but I do encourage you to work through the following summaries of chords and right-hand strumming and picking styles as a way of testing that you have really completed the course. I have only included chords introduced in the manual. For a more comprehensive list consult the guitar chord chart at the back of *Songs of Fellowship*.

Step 1: Summary of chords; test yourself

Below you will find twelve groups of chords, each related to a particular key. *Only* after you have tried to play through each group should you check yourself by referring to the identical group drawn in diagrams on the next pages. To make it more realistic as an assessment, give yourself a mark for every correct chord you manage without looking.

1.	C	C7	CM7	C2	Cdim	Cm	
2.	C#	C#m					
3.	D	D7	DM7	Dsus4	D6	Dm	D at fret 5
4.	Eb						
5.	E	E7	Esus4	E6	Em	Em7	
6.	F	FM7	Fm				
7.	F#	F#m					
8.	G	G7	Gsus4	G6	GM7		
9.	G#	G#m					
10.	A	A7	Asus4	A6	AM7	A at fret 5	Am
11.	Bb	BbM7					
12.	B	B7	Baug	Bm			

Possible score is 47. Well done if you achieved 35 or over. Try again if you got under 20 correct.

Please note that these chords are the ones introduced as part of this course.

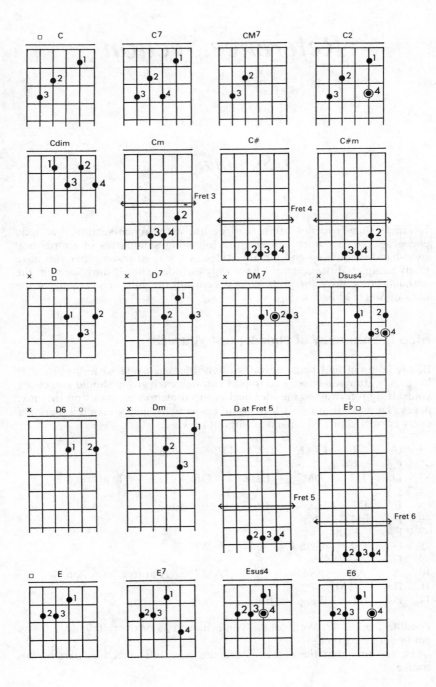

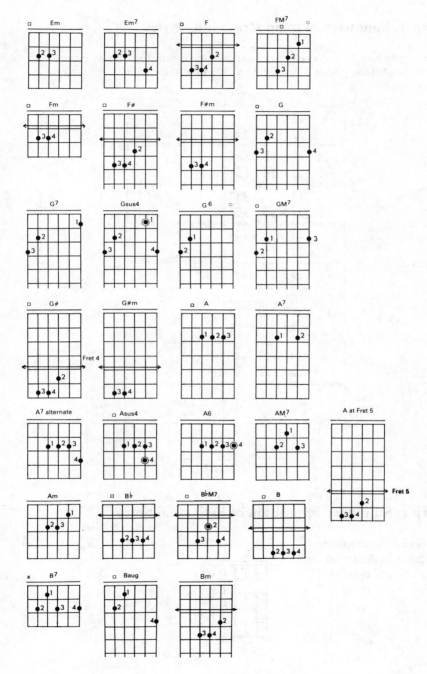

Step 2: Summary of main strumming styles

See if you can follow each series playing each one four times before you move on. Check yourself this time by listening to the tape.

	1	2	3	4	Session in which taught
a.	↓ ♩	↓↑ ♫	↓ ♩	↓↑ ♫	2
b.	↓ ♩	↓↑ ♫	↓↓ ♫	↓↑ ♫	7 and 8
c. 'Clock' Strum	PL PL ♫	↓↑ ♫	PL PL ♫	↓↑ ♫	9
d. Syncopated Strum	↓ ♩	↓↑ ♫	↑ ♫	↓↑ ♫	12
e.	↓↑ ♫	↓↓↑↑ ♬	↓↓ ♫	↓↑ ♫	18
f.	↓↑ ♩	↓↑↓↑ ♬	↓↓ ♫	↓↑↓↑ ♬	18
g.	↓ ♩	↓↑ ♫	↓↓↓ (3)	↓↑ ♫	17
h. 3-beat Strum		¹ Pick ♩	² ↓↑ ♫	³ ↓↑ ♫	3 and 17

Summary 2

Step 1: Summary of position of individual notes

1. Name the following notes as drawn on the fretboard diagram:

1 =

2 =

3 =

4 =

5 =

2. Draw in the positions of the following notes:

           (a) E on the D string
           (b) C# on the B string
           (c) G on the E string
           (d) A on the G string

Check your answers
from this full diagram:

3. Play the following phrases. They are all the beginning of well-known hymns or songs.

Step 2: Summary of picking styles

There are three groups given. The first group is suitable for songs with two beats in a bar (top figure 2 in a time signature), but are more often used played twice a bar in 4-beat songs. The second group is for 3-beat songs when a longer sequence is needed. The last group is for 4-beat songs.

Group one: $\frac{2}{4}$ *time*   *Group two:* $\frac{3}{4}$ *time*   *Group three:* $\frac{4}{4}$ *time*

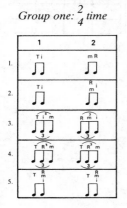

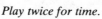

Play twice for time.

Time values of notes

NOTE			REST
𝅝	= Count 4	A whole note or semibreve	▬
𝅗𝅥	= Count 2	A half note or minim.	▬
𝅘𝅥	= Count 1	A quarter note or crotchet	𝄽
𝅘𝅥𝅮	= Count ½	An eighth note or quaver	𝄾
	Note: A dot after a note 𝅘𝅥. adds ½ the value of the note. So this note 𝅗𝅥. gets 3 counts.		

Names of notes

E   F   G   A   B   C   D   E

These eight are the ones you will mostly meet. Note that after G in music you return to the letter A.

Guitar strings in music

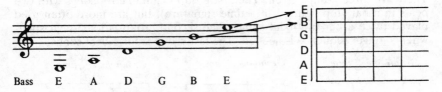

Bass   E   A   D   G   B   E

Five common scales

1. Scale C major (no sharps or flats)

Notes:	C	D	E	F	G	A	B	C
String:	5	open	4	4	open	3	open	2
Fret:	3	D	2	3	G	2	B	1

On the guitar fretboard the same scale

...open string B
...open string G
...open string D

2. Scale G major (has an F#)

Notes:	G	A	B	C	D	E	Fsharp	G

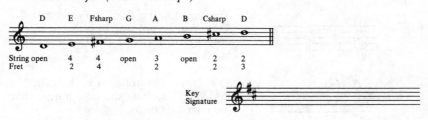

| String | open | 3 | open | 2 | 2 | open | 1 | 1 |
| Fret | | 2 | | 1 | 3 | | 2 | 3 |

Key Signature for G major:

3. Scale D major (has two sharps)

	D	E	Fsharp	G	A	B	Csharp	D

| String | open | 4 | 4 | open | 3 | open | 2 | 2 |
| Fret | | 2 | 4 | | 2 | | 2 | 3 |

Key Signature

4. Scale A major (has three sharps)

	A	B	Csharp	D	E	Fsharp	Gsharp	A

| String | 3 | open | 2 | 2 | open | 1 | 1 | 1 |
| Fret | 2 | | 2 | 3 | | 2 | 4 | 5 |

Key Signature

5. Scale E major (has four sharps)

	E	Fsharp	Gsharp	A	B	Csharp	Dsharp	E

| String | 4 | 4 | 3 | 3 | open | 2 | 2 | open |
| Fret | 2 | 4 | 1 | 2 | | 2 | 4 | |

Key Signature

The Shorthand of Music

Music is a fascinating language with its own signs and symbols. Here are some of the more common shorthand signs you will meet.

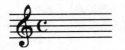

The letter C stands for COMMON TIME or 4 beats in a bar because this is the most common time in music.

Sharps or flats after the treble clef are a key signature. They tell you in which key the song is. This key signature is D major and every F and every C will be a sharp.

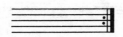

This is a repeat sign and you play or sing the song again from the beginning or from previous dots.

The line joining the 2 notes is called a TIE. You do not sing or play the second note again but hold the first one for 4 beats.

The little umbrella sign is called a PAUSE. You hold the note longer than the normal 4 beats.

E/B

This means that you play the chord of E major but the bass note is to be B. On the guitar this would be the note lying under your chord shape on the A string.

Fine

This is Latin for 'The end'.

F (E) Capo 1

An instruction for the guitarist. The music requires the sound of F major but you can use a capo at the first fret, play the E major shape and get the same sound.

The little sign over the note means you accent it.